Cambridge

Elements in American Politics
edited by
Frances E. Lee
Princeton University

WHY BAD POLICIES SPREAD (AND GOOD ONES DON'T)

Charles R. Shipan
University of Michigan

Craig Volden
University of Virginia

CAMBRIDGE
UNIVERSITY PRESS

CAMBRIDGE
UNIVERSITY PRESS

University Printing House, Cambridge CB2 8BS, United Kingdom

One Liberty Plaza, 20th Floor, New York, NY 10006, USA

477 Williamstown Road, Port Melbourne, VIC 3207, Australia

314–321, 3rd Floor, Plot 3, Splendor Forum, Jasola District Centre, New Delhi – 110025, India

103 Penang Road, #05–06/07, Visioncrest Commercial, Singapore 238467

Cambridge University Press is part of the University of Cambridge.

It furthers the University's mission by disseminating knowledge in the pursuit of education, learning, and research at the highest international levels of excellence.

www.cambridge.org
Information on this title: www.cambridge.org/9781009100304
DOI: 10.1017/9781108956123

First published 2021

A catalogue record for this publication is available from the British Library.

ISBN 978-1-009-10030-4 Hardback
ISBN 978-1-108-95836-3 Paperback
ISSN 2515-1606 (online)
ISSN 2515-1592 (print)

Cambridge University Press has no responsibility for the persistence or accuracy of URLs for external or third-party internet websites referred to in this publication and does not guarantee that any content on such websites is, or will remain, accurate or appropriate.

Why Bad Policies Spread (and Good Ones Don't)

Elements in American Politics

DOI: 10.1017/9781108956123
First published online: September 2021

Charles R. Shipan
University of Michigan

Craig Volden
University of Virginia

Author for correspondence: Charles R. Shipan, cshipan@umich.edu

Abstract: Building on a deep theoretical foundation and drawing on numerous examples, we examine how policies spread across the US states. We argue that for good policies to spread while bad policies are pushed aside, states must learn from one another. The three ingredients for this positive outcome are observable experiments, time to learn, and favorable incentives and expertise among policymakers. Although these ingredients are sometimes plentiful, we also note causes for concern, such as when policies are complex or incompatible with current practices, when policymakers give in to underlying political biases, or when political institutions lack the capacity for cultivating expertise. Under such conditions, states may rely on competition, imitation, and coercion, rather than learning, which can allow bad policies, rather than good ones, to spread. We conclude with lessons for reformers and policymakers and an assessment of our overall argument based on states' responses to the COVID-19 pandemic.

Keywords: American politics, federalism, policy diffusion, public policy, state politics

ISBNs: 9781009100304 (HB), 9781108958363 (PB), 9781108956123 (OC)
ISSNs: 2515-1606 (online), 2515-1592 (print)

Contents

1 The Laboratories of Democracy

1.1 COVID-19 and the US States

In late 2019, reports began to circulate about a new and worrisome virus that had emerged in the Chinese city of Wuhan. Chinese authorities initially downplayed the severity of the situation; however, by the end of December, they acknowledged the existence of a large cluster of viral pneumonia cases in Wuhan. Although the specific source of these illnesses was unknown, health officials discovered that many of those stricken had ties to Wuhan's Huanan Seafood Market, so they shut down this market on January 1, 2020. Still, initial reports from the World Health Organization (WHO) a week later contended that there was no evidence of human-to-human transmission of whatever virus was causing these illnesses.[1]

At first, this outbreak received limited attention in the United States. The cluster of cases appeared to be localized. The outbreak was in a far-off city that few Americans had even heard of, despite a population of 11 million people – the size of New York City and Chicago combined. The United States had been spared the effects of earlier outbreaks from similar viruses such as SARS in 2003 and MERS in 2012. Furthermore, some political leaders and health officials in the United States initially downplayed the extent to which this new virus might be contagious.

Then the situation changed quickly; on January 21, the US Centers for Disease Control and Prevention (CDC) acknowledged the first known case of the virus in the United States.[2] Major US airports began to screen passengers coming from China on January 17, but the infected person had traveled from Wuhan to Washington State on January 15. The coronavirus, which would be named SARS-CoV-2 and which produced the disease that came to be designated COVID-19, was now officially in the United States. By the end of January – only one month after the *New York Times* first wrote about a "mystery pneumonia-like illness"[3] in China – the CDC reported the first case of person-to-person transmission of the coronavirus in the United States, and the WHO labeled the outbreak a "public health emergency of international concern."[4]

Much has been written about the US federal government's hesitant and inconsistent response to the emergence of the coronavirus. The focus of this

---

[1] www.who.int/csr/don/05-january-2020-pneumonia-of-unkown-cause-china/en/ As of summer 2021, investigators remained uncertain whether the virus emerged from animal-to-human transmission or via a leak from a research laboratory.

[2] Later analysis suggested the virus might have been circulating in the United States in late 2019.

[3] www.nytimes.com/2020/01/06/world/asia/china-SARS-pneumonialike.html

[4] See www.nytimes.com/article/coronavirus-timeline.html for a useful timeline.

study, however, is not on the federal government but rather on how state governments make public policy. Consider the situation in which states unexpectedly found themselves with respect to COVID-19. In February, California, Oregon, and Washington announced new cases of the disease. Then in the first week of March, the number of cases and the number of states with cases rapidly began to escalate. In the first four days of March, Arizona, New York, North Carolina, and New Hampshire all announced their first cases, followed by Nevada, Tennessee, Colorado, and Maryland the next day, and ten more states the day after that. Nearly every US state found itself confronting the outbreak of a lethal virus, one that virtually no one had heard of only a few weeks earlier.

Policymakers in every state immediately found themselves needing to make decisions on a range of issues. Should they attempt to restrict people living in harder-hit states from traveling to their state? How could they procure the personal protective equipment (PPE) needed by frontline medical workers? Given the shortages of such equipment, how should they ration it? Should they shut down K-12 schools – and if so, temporarily or for the remainder of the school year? Should athletic events be canceled? Who should be eligible to get tested for the virus? What protections should be adopted for the most at-risk people, such as those living in nursing homes? State leaders were abruptly faced with a seemingly endless list of critical decisions, all of which needed to be addressed as soon as possible.

As a crucial first step, policymakers – in most cases, governors, with input from legislators and public health officials – had to decide whether to issue stay-at-home orders. The working hypothesis behind these orders was that keeping people at home would limit everyone's exposure to those who already had contracted the disease. And this in turn would "flatten the curve" by reducing the number of new infections and hospitalizations.[5] That is, preventive actions would distribute the incidence of the disease over a longer period of time, which in turn would help hospitals avoid becoming overwhelmed. This hypothesis was plausible and was supported by most experts, but it was theoretical, with little evidence of how successful it would be or how best to implement it. In addition, it would come at a significant economic cost, with businesses closing and millions of workers being laid off.

With the virus spreading rapidly, cases increasing dramatically, and deaths beginning to mount, policymakers had little time to figure out the best course of action. In mid-March, within days of one another, governors in all fifty states issued "state of emergency" declarations to enhance their powers to combat the

---

[5] The phrase "flatten the curve" and the logic behind this idea are usually attributed to Howard Markel, a professor and physician at the University of Michigan. See Kruzel 2020.

coronavirus. Starting with California, states then began to issue directives ordering their citizens to remain in their homes. On March 30, within hours of one another, Virginia, Maryland, and the District of Columbia all issued stay-at-home orders. By April 2, thirty-eight states had imitated the actions of those first adopters. In seven more states, local officials adopted such a policy. Only a handful of states – Arkansas, Iowa, Nebraska, North Dakota, and South Dakota – chose not to implement such policies either statewide or locally.

Figure 1 captures the remarkable speed of the adoption of stay-at-home orders. In a little more than two weeks, we moved from a single state taking this action to a large majority having done so, a strikingly fast spread of such a major and intrusive policy. Were these stay-at-home orders likely to work? It seemed plausible that they would; but with such an intense need to act quickly, there was little time for states to carefully assess the effectiveness of such orders and little incentive to delay action until experts could conduct such assessments. Furthermore, there was little evidence regarding the specific form the orders should take – whether they should apply to everyone in the state, to pockets of the state that were at higher risk, to only specific categories of nonessential workers, and so on. Nor was there any certainty about how negatively these laws would affect the economy. Yet there was no time to wait and learn from

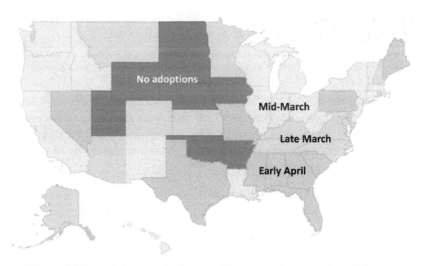

Figure 1 The quick spread of statewide stay-at-home orders (March–April 2020). Data for figure compiled from "States' COVID-19 Public Health Emergency Declarations, Mask Requirements and Travel Advisories," National Academy for State Health Policy (www.nashp.org/governors-prioritize-health-for-all/).

other states' experiments. States needed to move quickly; once some acted, others followed in short order.

Another front in state-level responses to the virus concerned whether states should require citizens to wear face masks when going out in public. This policy question emerged later and followed a different, slower pattern than that for stay-at-home orders. Only a few states required face masks initially; some that did, such as Ohio, quickly reversed the policy when citizens reacted negatively to the order.

Throughout the spring of 2020, however, evidence about the effectiveness of wearing masks steadily began to mount. This evidence took many forms[6] – laboratory tests on animals demonstrated that masks were effective in reducing contagion; computer simulations showed the virus could be nearly eradicated in the United States if approximately 70 percent of the public would wear masks; countries in which mask wearing was the norm (such as Japan[7]) were faring far better than those without such practices. Still, few states issued full or even partial mandates for mask wearing.

One reason US states hesitated to mandate masks was concern about the public's reaction. In general, polls and observed behaviors showed that strong majorities of the public supported wearing masks, but they also revealed stark partisan differences. Republicans (focused on individual liberty costs) were much less likely than Democrats (focused on community health benefits) to wear masks or to support a mask mandate, with independents falling in between. As a result, state policymakers had to worry about the political costs of issuing such an order, particularly since 2020 was an election year.

Conflicting signals from the national government contributed to the lack of action on mask policies. On February 29, 2020, US Surgeon General Jerome Adams tweeted:

> Seriously people – STOP BUYING MASKS! They are NOT effective in preventing general public from catching #Coronavirus, but if healthcare providers can't get them to care for sick patients, it puts them and our communities at risk!

At the time, US citizens were advised to wear masks only if they felt sick or were at high risk. Once evidence began to emerge of a surprisingly high number

---

[6] See www.nature.com/articles/d41586-020-02801-8 and www.vanityfair.com/news/2020/05/masks-covid-19-infections-would-plummet-new-study-says.

[7] Despite being a country with a much older population living in densely packed cities – both of which would portend a significant outbreak – and despite not shutting down the economy (and not even closing virus incubators like karaoke bars), the death rate from the virus in Japan as of July 2020 was one-*fiftieth* of that in the United States. Many experts attributed this outcome in large part to the universal norm of wearing masks in public in Japan (www.bbc.com/news/world-asia-53188847). Other Southeast Asian countries in which mask wearing was the norm, like Thailand, also suffered far fewer infections and casualties in the early months of the pandemic.

of asymptomatic disease spreaders, however, the CDC shifted gears and advised people to wear masks in public places. But signals remained mixed. On the one hand, public health experts like Dr. Anthony Fauci, who originally had said that masks were not necessary ("There's no reason to be walking around with a mask"), now started to encourage people to wear masks (and to wear one himself).[8] First Lady Melania Trump signaled her support for the CDC's new guidance. On the other hand, President Donald Trump, while acknowledging the CDC's recommendation, said, "This is voluntary. I don't think I'm going to be doing it." Vice President Mike Pence, following the president's lead, did not wear a mask while touring the Mayo Clinic in April to observe their work with COVID-19 patients (an action for which he later apologized).

Faced with these mixed signals both from citizens within their states and from national political leaders, state policymakers varied considerably in their masking policies and prescriptions. By June, a combination of changing policy outcomes and emerging evidence offered newfound clarity. First, in terms of policy effects, a number of states chose to reopen their economies, even before reaching CDC-recommended benchmarks for doing so. As a result, the virus started to spread out of control again, with some states like Arizona, Florida, and Texas hit especially hard and fourteen states seeing record numbers of cases by the end of June. With the pandemic becoming ever more salient and spreading to new places, state policymakers were looking for policy options that promised to control the virus.

Second, national political leaders, including prominent Republican members of Congress like Senate Majority Leader Mitch McConnell, Senator Chuck Grassley, Senator Lamar Alexander, House Minority Leader Kevin McCarthy, and Representative Liz Cheney, began to advocate more strongly and consistently for wearing masks, as did well-known Fox News personality Sean Hannity.[9] Even President Trump occasionally struck a different tone, at one point saying "I'm all for masks" and allowing himself to be photographed wearing a mask for the first time in mid-July. Support from these high-profile Republicans and conservatives was especially important for governors who worried about the political costs of a mask mandate, given the opposition among a substantial number of Republican voters.

Third, and for our purposes most importantly, evidence about the efficacy of masks began to emerge not just from abstract scientific studies or from other

---

[8] See www.reuters.com/article/uk-factcheck-fauci-outdated-video-masks/fact-checkoutdated-video-of-fauci-saying-theres-no-reason-to-be-walking-around-with-a-mask-idUSKBN26T2TR.

[9] www.washingtonpost.com/politics/republican-leaders-now-say-everyone-should-wear-a-mask–even-as-trump-refuses-and-mocks-those-who-do/2020/06/30/995a32d0-bae9-11ea-80b9-40ece9a701dc_story.html

countries but also from other states, which had begun to experiment with mask-wearing policies. Some of this evidence was anecdotal: several of the earliest places that had been hardest hit, such as New York City, had brought the virus under control in part through embracing mask wearing. Other more systematic studies supported this conclusion, showing that mandates caused more people to wear masks, a behavioral change that yielded a significant reduction of cases and deaths. One scientific study estimated that the mask requirement implemented by fifteen states between April 8 and May 15 led to a decrease of between 230,000 and 450,000 cases in those states.[10]

By early July 2020, several more states had adopted mandates, including some that previously had argued against doing so but changed their view after assessing outcomes in states with mask mandates.[11] As Figure 2 shows, mask

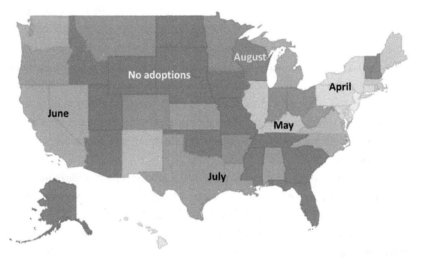

Figure 2 The slower spread of statewide mask mandates (April–August 2020). Data for figure compiled from "States' COVID-19 Public Health Emergency Declarations, Mask Requirements and Travel Advisories," National Academy for State Health Policy (www.nashp.org/governors-prioritize-health-for-all/).

---

[10] See www.healthaffairs.org/doi/10.1377/hlthaff.2020.00818. Goldman Sachs also conducted a study about the efficacy of masks in mid-summer 2020, concluding at the time that "Our numerical estimates are that cumulative cases grow 17.3 percent per week without a mask mandate but only 7.3 percent with a mask mandate, and that cumulative fatalities grow 29 percent per week without a mask mandate but only 16 percent with a mask mandate." The study further estimated that a universal mask mandate would save 5 percent of GDP. See www.washingtonpost.com/business/2020/06/30/mask-mandate-gdp-economy-goldman-sachs/.

[11] For example, Texas Governor Greg Abbott, who earlier refused to issue a state-level mask mandate and blocked local governments from mandating masks, partially reversed course, ordering anyone in a Texas county adversely affected by the virus to wear a mask in public.

mandates – like stay-at-home orders – spread across the states, but they did so more slowly. Only a few states experimented with mandates in April, but over time states were able to observe more and more experiments with mask mandates and to take the time to learn about the effects of these experiments. By August, the majority of states had adopted this policy. Not all states issued mask mandates (a point we return to later), but many did, after gauging whether or not the adoption of this policy would help in their state.

As this brief overview of state responses to the first several months of COVID-19 in the United States indicates, we sometimes see quick convergence to specific policies across almost all the states, as occurred with stay-at-home orders. In other instances, states do not converge, and those adopting a new policy take longer to do so. In still other areas – such as COVID-19 policies regarding aid to unemployed workers, determining who was eligible for testing or vaccines, reopening restaurants and bars, and so on – we continued to see a patchwork of different policies throughout the pandemic.

This variety of outcomes indicates the complicated nature of policymaking in a federal system, with policy choices affected by public opinion, political parties, current events, and more. But it also indicates that state choices can be influenced by observing what other states have done, taking time to consider those other actions, and then assessing them. In other words, within American federalism, states can *learn* from one another, resulting in the spread of good policies. But do they? Which policies spread for which reasons? Which conditions lead good policies (and not bad ones) to spread, or vice versa? These questions form the central focus of this study.

1.2 Policymaking in the US Federal System

The ability of different states to experiment with different policies – to act as policy laboratories – is one of the foundational promises of our government's federal construction. This experimentation can then lead to the discovery of new policies, ones that are more innovative and, by some criteria, better. Furthermore, with states approaching a policy from various angles, other states can observe these earlier approaches and decide whether or not to adopt them. In this way, a federal system can allow for good policies to spread while limiting the spread of bad policies.

That, at least, is the ideal in a federal system. By allowing states to experiment with different policies, we can discover which policies work and which ones do not. Later-adopting states can observe which policies worked – and where, and why, and how – thereby facilitating the spread of good policies while containing bad ones. But an unanswered question is whether state policymaking in our federal system actually operates this way in practice. This study explores whether that ideal holds, whether our federal structure of policymaking does indeed facilitate the spread of good policies while constraining the spread of bad ones.

Before proceeding, we first need to address what we mean by "good" and "bad" policies. We recognize, of course, that these are value-laden terms, and that what one person views as a good policy another might view as a bad one. To choose just one example, a religious conservative might view a policy that restricts access to abortion as a good one, whereas a secular liberal might view that same policy as a bad one. Thus, defining "good" and "bad" policies is not always straightforward. Policy analysts have long struggled with what constitutes a good policy, and we won't resolve this difficulty here.[12] What we can do is set out guidelines that we – and those interested in state policymaking – can use.

We begin with the classic definition based on benefit-cost analysis, which suggests that a good policy is one in which the benefits of the policy outweigh the costs. Yet because there have been few systematic cost-benefit analyses of policies across all fifty states, we embrace a somewhat broader definition of good policies that also includes those in which the policy successfully achieves the goals it sets out to accomplish and those policies that embody best practices.[13] This definition can be applied in many policy areas, beyond only those assessed by the most rigorous cost-benefit analyses.

This view of what constitutes a good policy also allows that different states might use different evaluative criteria when designing and evaluating a policy.[14] With respect to COVID-19 policies, for example, a state might choose to emphasize protecting the health of its citizens as the primary goal of any potential policy. Other states might instead focus on protecting the economy. Or they might attempt to strike a balance between health and the economy. Or they might emphasize other goals, such as ensuring individual liberty or access to in-person education. Moreover, some considerations – like COVID-19 cases and deaths – may be easier to measure and therefore may become more salient

---

[12] McConnell (2010) identifies the difficulties involved in characterizing a policy as good or bad and argues that many policies may succeed along some dimensions but not others.

[13] As such, we are not engaged in a hypothetical exercise, wherein the best available policy is later declared bad because something better has come along (although an insistence on keeping a mediocre policy when a much better one appears may be considered bad policymaking).

[14] This is not to suggest that whatever policymakers embrace should be deemed "good public policy." Often what is politically expedient has significant longer-term consequences. Failing to address climate change or ignoring budget deficits, while politically beneficial in the short run, ultimately has costs, and often those costs grow substantially over time. The bill always comes due.

than other criteria or values.[15] Each state can decide how much weight to place on each of the many dimensions of policy when determining its goals and assessing the effects of its policy choices.[16] Such state-by-state variance, if responsive to the values held by its citizens, tends to be better than a one-size-fits-all approach.

In evaluating a policy, it is also worth recognizing that although a good policy might achieve the goals its proponents promised, those benefits may be short-lived or dependent on further policy choices. The Czech Republic, for example, was one of the early success stories with respect to COVID-19, quickly adopting and promoting a universal mask-wearing policy and seeing a dramatic reduction in infections. However, in response to this initial success, the country then followed this first policy choice with other policy choices, such as opening up the economy too soon and promoting tourism, that undermined its successes and soon led to some of the worst outcomes during the pandemic.[17] Thus, when we discuss whether a policy is good, we are talking about whether that policy had its intended, positive effect, regardless of whether or not later policy choices undercut that effect. Conversely, initially troubling policy choices can be modified and improved by governments that continue to learn beyond their original adoption.[18]

Taken together, good policies are ones that provide more benefits than costs, in line with the goals of the policies' proponents, while also recognizing that different states will weigh policy costs and benefits differently and that initial success does not guarantee continued success. We believe this definition of good and bad policies strikes the right balance between being too vague and too restrictive.[19]

Our goal is to understand whether, in our federal system, good policies spread while bad ones don't. As the title of this study suggests, we contend that good

---

[15] Depending on whether they are conducted by independent bureaucrats, elected policymakers, or interested policy advocates, policy analyses likewise vary in the measurements used and the weights attached to particular evaluative criteria.

[16] Gilardi, Shipan, and Wüest (2021) demonstrate how different states emphasize different aspects of policies.

[17] This example illustrates both that there is a time dimension to evaluating policies and that in addition to individual policies, combinations of policies might be necessary to ensure success. We develop this second point in more detail in Section 2.

[18] Glick (2012) explores the trade-off between mimicking and modifying.

[19] Adding further complexity to the idea of good or bad policy choices is that the same policy that is good for one state may be bad for another state, depending on its circumstances and the weights it chooses to place on different evaluative criteria. We return to this idea when we discuss the concepts of "trialability" and "relative advantage." Furthermore, when policy choices are made not by weighing costs and benefits but instead are based on undue partisan political pressures or electoral concerns, fears of appearing weak or indecisive, or wishful thinking rather than concrete evidence, bad policy outcomes are more likely to follow. Good politics and good policy are not necessarily aligned.

policies often do *not* spread, while bad ones might. However, our perspective is not all doom and gloom, as we also identify the conditions, lessons, and reform proposals that allow good policies to spread and that can hinder the spread of bad policies. Doing so requires us to think systematically about why policies spread, a task to which we now turn.

1.3 Policy Diffusion

State legislators often seek office because of their interest in a specific policy. One legislator might be interested primarily in agricultural issues, perhaps because they grew up on a farm. Another might be drawn to issues that revolve around the provision of insurance, perhaps because of a prior life experience or because insurance issues are highly salient in their district – say, due to increased risks for fires or floods. Still others might feel most passionate about civil rights issues, or education, or small businesses.

These legislators can specialize and gain policy expertise in their preferred issue areas once they are elected to office. But they also will find themselves dealing with issues that extend well beyond their own personal interests or those of their constituents. The legislator who sought public service to influence insurance policy ends up participating in hearings related to roads and transportation. The one who became a legislator to reform agriculture policy winds up voting on bills dealing with Medicaid requirements or racial injustice. Sometimes policymakers have the choice of which issues they will address. However, as the spread of COVID-19 illustrates, other policy issues often force their way onto the agenda. Policymakers need to tackle them just the same.

Faced with a wide range of issues, state legislators have to figure out which policy actions to take. In large part, they do this by considering factors that are internal to the state. In setting a new policy related to crime, for example, legislators might be influenced by the overall level of crime in their state and the type of criminal activity that occurs most frequently (whether violent, property, or white-collar crime). They might also consider the public's perception about whether crime has been worsening, public opinion toward policing and incarceration, and a variety of demographic factors in the state, such as population density in its cities, the distributions of age and education among state residents, and so on.

State policymakers also can be influenced by *external* factors. More specifically, they can observe what other states have done to address a policy problem and then take this information into account when deciding whether to act and if so what action to take. If state legislators in Wisconsin are deciding what crime policy to enact, they can look to see which actions have been successful (or not) in Minnesota. Legislators in Alabama might view Georgia as a leader in promoting economic development and thus be influenced by policies found there. Iowa might choose to pass a law limiting smoking in restaurants that is no stronger than Nebraska's, if there is a concern that Council Bluffs will lose business across the river to Omaha. And several states might choose to enact specific health insurance policies because of incentives the federal government provides.

In all of these cases, the policy that a state chooses to implement is influenced, at least in part, by prior policy adoptions in other states. This process, in which the decisions of earlier policy adopters influence those of later adopters, is known as *policy diffusion*. Policy diffusion arises when state policymaking is *interdependent*, rather than independent, with policies spreading across the states. State legislatures do not ignore the sorts of internal factors identified earlier, but they also do not make policy decisions purely independently, ignoring activity that happens outside of their borders.

For several decades now, political scientists have asked: do public policies diffuse across the states? In study after study, evidence of diffusion has accumulated.[20] There is disagreement about exactly how or why policies spread, or which states are more likely to lead or to follow, or whether certain sorts of policies are more likely to diffuse than others. However, on the most general point – whether policies diffuse – the answer is a clear and unequivocal "yes." Public policies diffuse, or spread, across the US states.

It is not just a small set of policies that diffuse, or certain types of policies, such as morality or economic policies. Instead, scholars have found evidence of policy diffusion across a strikingly broad range of policies, including state lotteries, tax increases, gaming on Indian lands, thermal insulation in new home construction, lien laws, welfare, fair employment practices, right to die issues, living will laws, education, civil rights, child abuse reporting laws, crime victim compensation, abortion, tobacco and smoking, school choice, clean air programs, health insurance policies, and electricity sector regulation. And that's just a partial list! Again, the bottom line is that when states create new policies, their choices are influenced not just by factors internal to the states – demographics, ideologies, political institutions, interest groups, and so on. Their choices also are influenced by actions that other states have taken.

Furthermore, there is general agreement about the *mechanisms* that produce diffusion. If Alabama is more likely to adopt an economic development policy because Georgia has done so, what are the broad factors that caused Alabama to

---

[20] Pathbreaking early studies include Walker (1969) and Gray (1973). For more recent overviews of the literature on policy diffusion, see Graham, Shipan, and Volden (2013), LaCombe and Boehmke (2020), and especially Mooney (2020).

act in this way? If Maine adopts a policy regarding state parks after Idaho does so, what prompted Maine to do this? These mechanisms represent an attempt to explain the causes of diffusion, to identify the process through which a state's policy choices become interdependent with those of earlier adopting states.

Scholars have posited and shown that four main mechanisms produce diffusion: learning, imitation, competition, and coercion.[21] These mechanisms can occur in isolation, or they can occur in tandem, and they help explain why policies can, and do, spread from one state to another. As we shall see, these explanations of why policies spread – of the paths that they take – end up telling us a lot about whether good policies and bad policies might or might not spread.

One normatively appealing possibility is that policies diffuse because states *learn* from the actions of earlier adopters. Imagine that a state is considering whether or not to revamp its immigration policies. In particular, it is trying to decide whether or not to place restrictions on unauthorized migrants – that is, people who are in the state without having gone through the required procedures for being in the state legally. There certainly are internal factors that state policymakers will take into account, such as the unemployment rate, the crime rate, if the agricultural sector or other businesses benefit from the work these migrants provide, public attitudes toward immigrants, the strength of pro- and anti-immigration groups in the state, and so on. But this state can also look at the experiences of other states that have addressed the issue of unauthorized immigration. How did the unemployment rate change following their adoption of new immigration policies? What was the public's reaction to these policies – was there a backlash, or was the public generally supportive? How did this reaction vary by partisan attachment? Did the estimated number of unauthorized migrants decrease? Was there less strain on public services once the policy was enacted? If the action these states took was in line with the preferences and goals of the federal government, did the state find itself receiving additional benefits and top-down support?

In other words, state policymakers can observe the full range of outcomes found in states that already have adopted policies, including good and bad outcomes and information about how well such policies fit with their own circumstances. Based on these observations, states can learn from the experiences of other states and decide which policy or policies to enact – or whether or not to enact a new policy. This does not imply that a state merely mimics others with no regard for its own prior experiences and beliefs. Instead, policymakers build on these existing beliefs, updating them based on what they observe in other states.[22]

---

[21] See Shipan and Volden (2008) and Maggetti and Gilardi (2016).

[22] This type of learning, where prior beliefs are updated based on new observations, is known as "Bayesian updating." A critique of this approach to policy diffusion contends that rational updating demands too much of decision-makers and that policymakers instead are *boundedly*

We will argue that diffusion mechanisms other than learning tend to pull states away from adopting good policies and push them toward making mistakes. Consider, for example, *imitation*, sometimes also called "emulation" or "mimicry." With imitation, a state that is considering a policy adoption observes what an earlier state or states have done and then takes a similar action regardless of that policy's consequences or applicability. Perhaps an early adopter has a reputation for being at the cutting edge in a specific policy area – for example, California in the area of environmental policy.[23] Other states observe the policy that California has enacted, believing that any policy good enough for California (with its vast expertise regarding environmental policy and its outsized influence over what companies do) will be good enough for them, too. Or maybe acting on environmental issues is normatively appealing to some states, where it just seems like the right thing to do. Regardless of the reason, a failure to invest in learning means that imitation – copying without waiting to discern the policies' effects – is a gamble.

Another potentially problematic diffusion mechanism is *competition*, in which a state adopts a policy based on economic rivalries with other states. For example, states may worry that if they set taxes too high, they might lose businesses and residents to other states. As a result, they may set taxes too low, leading to underfunding of important services.[24] They similarly might fear that businesses will leave if environmental or labor standards are too strict. As another example, policymakers compete with one another to attract filmmaking to their states by providing production companies with incentives to film in their states, hoping that the jobs and positive publicity outweigh the costs of such incentives.[25] Competition is likewise present in attempts to attract corporate headquarters or distribution centers to a state. Sometimes these competitive pressures push states away from the (good) policies they would prefer in the absence of such competition. In the extreme, they engage in a mutually destructive "race to the bottom."[26]

Finally, policies can diffuse due to *coercion*. In comparative or international politics, coercion is fairly common, with larger or more powerful countries

---

rational, more limited in their ability to learn from earlier adopters (Meseguer 2006, Weyland 2007).

[23] Scholars increasingly have analyzed which states are leaders, with their policies quickly cascading to others (e.g., Boehmke and Skinner 2012). For example, Billard, Creti, and Mandel (2020) identify Minnesota, Florida, and Massachusetts as leaders on climate change.

[24] Berry and Berry (1992) explore tax competition and diffusion considerations.

[25] For example, for several years the state of Michigan drew film productions to the state by providing companies with tax credits and subsidies. See www.indiewire.com/2011/03/michigans-film-incentives-are-leaving-so-are-its-filmmakers-243152/

[26] Peterson and Rom (1990) and Volden (2002) examine race-to-the-bottom considerations in state welfare policies.

pressuring other countries to take specific actions. In the United States, state-to-state coercion is rare relative to coercion across levels of government. States can coerce local governments either to take specific actions or to *not* take specific actions, such as when some mayors wanted to implement pandemic mask-wearing requirements, but state government leaders prevented them from doing so.[27] Likewise, the national government can coerce states to take certain actions. In some cases, this can take the form of informal threats, such as when President Trump implied that he would not be willing to provide medical equipment needed to fight the coronavirus to states that did not "treat him well" and would also withhold federal coronavirus aid to states that pursued immigration policies he did not like, such as allowing sanctuary cities.[28] Such a heavy-handed approach, however, is unusual. More common is coercion through incentives that are baked into intergovernmental grant programs, such as the threatened removal of highway funds from states that did not set preferred speed limits or drinking ages.[29] Regardless of approach, coercion leads politicians to adopt policies that they otherwise would have dismissed as not in the best interests of their states.

1.4 Our Argument

When the national government is paralyzed by polarization and partisan politics, effective state policymaking becomes ever more important. Studies of diffusion help us understand that policies can, and do, spread from state to state. Furthermore, we know that policies can diffuse because states learn from one another. They also can spread because states imitate one another, are in competition, and sometimes are coerced into taking specific actions.

Will the process of diffusion work in the ideal way, where good policies spread, but bad ones will not? Or will we end up in the inverse situation, where bad policies spread, but good ones do not? We argue that although the diffusion of good policies is a possibility, it is not a certainty. A helpful factor for good policies to spread, we maintain, is that states are able to learn from initial policy experiments elsewhere. When learning is the mechanism by which policies

---

[27] For example, Arizona Governor Doug Ducey and Texas Governor Greg Abbott blocked local governments from creating mask mandates and did so for months before relenting in the face of pressure from medical and business leaders once their states started seeing dramatic increases in COVID-19 cases. Georgia Governor Brian Kemp also blocked local governments from requiring masks in public places and then sued Atlanta when that city's mayor, Keisha Lance Bottoms, defied his order by implementing a mask-wearing requirement.

[28] On threats regarding sanctuary cities, see www.businessinsider.com/trump-coronavirus-aid-threatens-to-withhold-states-sanctuary-cities-2020-4.

[29] Another route for the national government to influence states is by drawing attention to an issue. In so doing, it can get the states to act on this issue, even without passing new laws or using financial threats (Karch 2012; Clouser McCann, Shipan, and Volden 2015).

diffuse, there is a greater likelihood that good policies will spread and bad ones will die on the vine. For this to happen, political leaders in a state need to learn, for example, whether policy options will be politically viable and acceptable to citizens in their states. They need to discern whether these existing policies have been successful in terms of their policy consequences. And they need to determine how best to adapt policies found elsewhere for their own needs.

We contend that this kind of learning can, and does, take place, at least if certain conditions are met. Specifically, we argue that three ingredients offer the best recipe for the learning-based spread of good public policies. First, there must be observable experiments from which other states can learn. Second, states must have the time to learn from those experiments, identifying their costs and benefits over both the short and the long term. And third, states must have the incentives to engage in learning and have the expertise needed to carry out that learning effectively.

Although these three ingredients definitely exist in many states and for many policy problems, there are also many times when the recipe fails. Put simply, learning is hard. It is neither automatic nor guaranteed. As we will see, policies themselves often have features that can get in the way of learning. Some have effects that are difficult to observe, at least initially. Others are complex or are incompatible with the current conditions found in some states. Moreover, in choosing among these policies, policymakers are challenged by the same biases that all humans face. They rely too much on easily available information or solutions, get caught up in short-term thinking, and take positions that advance their career interests rather than good policy objectives. Furthermore, political institutions – sometimes under-funded, understaffed, or lacking informed policy entrepreneurs – can impede the spread of good policies.

Also presenting challenges for states to act as effective policy laboratories is our observation that policies can diffuse for reasons other than learning. Policies that spread due to imitation, competition, or coercion often can produce poor outcomes. Instead of learning, states might adopt policies because they are in competition with other states. Although competition can be beneficial in holding down costs or promoting innovation, it also can have negative effects, such as when business tax breaks end up costing the state more revenue than they generate. States also might adopt policies because they are merely imitating what earlier states have done, perhaps to appear innovative themselves or to seek legitimacy by associating themselves with these earlier states. When this occurs, states do not learn from these earlier adopters; rather, they simply copy what early adopters have done, without regard for whether the policy is successful or whether it is a good fit. Tough-on-crime measures provide an example of policies that were copied without learning; stay-at-home orders due to

COVID-19 also were adopted very quickly, before any learning could take place. Finally, coercion can cause states to grudgingly adopt policies that might not be appropriate within their borders. Not all policies that spread through these alternative mechanisms will lead to bad outcomes, nor does learning always produce good policy choices. But learning does make policy success much more likely.

We therefore set out to describe how diffusion can operate within a federal system; to explain how learning is helpful in achieving the positive outcomes predicted by those who extol the virtues of federalism; and to affirm that learning can, and does, occur. Having explained how the mechanism of learning can lead to good policies spreading and to the avoidance of bad ones, we then explore what can go wrong. We argue that features of both politics and policies themselves can hinder learning and that mechanisms other than learning can lead to the passage of policies that are less than ideal. Finally, this journey exploring the promise and perils of policy diffusion allows us to return to the concept of states as policy laboratories, with a better understanding of the lessons that state policymakers might learn and the reforms they could consider to help achieve the promise of American federalism.

2 The Promise: How Good Policies Can Spread (While Bad Ones Can Be Contained)

2.1 Learning How to Limit Youth Smoking

In 1995, David Kessler, the highly respected commissioner of the Food and Drug Administration (FDA), identified smoking as a pediatric disease.[30] Smoking is far more prevalent among adults than children, of course, so this might seem like an unusual way to characterize smoking. However, Kessler pointed out that thinking about smoking as an adult disease or even an adult problem ignored the origins of addiction to cigarettes. The vast majority of adults who are addicted to cigarettes began smoking when they were teenagers, whereas people who start after age 25 are much less likely to become addicted. Moreover, nearly three-quarters of teens who start smoking end up regretting it, with many unable to stop due to the addictive nature of nicotine. Given the increases in smoking rates among high school seniors and first-year college students during the late 1980s and early 1990s, Kessler was highlighting the need for government to take action to reduce smoking by youths.

Smoking, like many policy areas in the United States, falls under the purview of multiple levels of government. Which levels act, and in which ways, depends

---

[30] See www.nytimes.com/1995/03/09/us/fda-head-calls-smoking-a-pediatric-disease.html.

largely on politics. Given the influence of pro-tobacco groups over Congress, anti-smoking advocates turned to the federal bureaucracy and to states and localities. The FDA, for example, attempted to regulate smoking during Kessler's tenure as commissioner, but the Supreme Court ruled that the agency lacked congressional authorization to do so. It was not until 2009 that Congress passed the Federal Smoking Prevention and Tobacco Control Act, which finally gave the FDA the authority to regulate tobacco. Still, the vast majority of public policy decisions related to cigarettes, such as whether to allow or prohibit smoking in workplaces, bars, and restaurants, continue to fall to cities and states.

To complement (and coerce) state action, the national government used its financial power to push states to adopt anti-smoking policies targeted at young people.[31] In 1992, as part of the Alcohol, Drug Abuse, and Mental Health Administration Reorganization Act, Congress passed the Synar Amendment, which directed states to reduce the incidence of youth smoking within their borders. This law required states to set the minimum age for the purchase of tobacco products at age 18. But it also instructed states to take actions that made it more difficult for people younger than age 18 to purchase cigarettes, similar to the federal government's indirect pressure on states to raise the drinking age to 21 if they wished to avoid the loss of highway funds. The Synar Amendment did not tell states which specific laws they had to enact to reduce youth access to cigarettes. Instead, states were required to bring the rate at which underage people were able to purchase cigarettes to under 20 percent.[32] States that failed to do so or to make progress toward this goal would forfeit up to 40 percent of the Substance Abuse Prevention and Treatment block grant that they received from the federal government, a significant loss of revenue for most states.

Because of the Synar Amendment, states suddenly found themselves needing to adopt policies making it harder for teenagers to purchase cigarettes, with the ultimate goal of lowering youth smoking rates. In some states, both smoking rates and the rates at which youths were able to purchase cigarettes were high; in others, they were low. Surveys revealed that teenage cigarette use in the mid-1990s ranged from 17 percent in Utah to 43 percent in West Virginia.[33] Initial youth access studies showed the ability of teenagers to successfully purchase cigarettes exceeded 40 percent in most states, with rates as high as 73 percent in Louisiana.

---

[31] Even though pro-tobacco groups were able to use their considerable power at the national level to block most anti-smoking laws, it was difficult, to say the least, for them to mount a case in favor of youth smoking.

[32] In other words, states had to show that when people younger than age 18 tried to purchase cigarettes, they were successful less than 20 percent of the time. States essentially had to conduct sting operations, where they would send young people into stores to try to purchase cigarettes. States then had to report the percentage of purchase attempts that were successful.

[33] These statistics come from the 1995 Youth Risk Behavior Surveillance System (YRBSS).

Which policies should states adopt to bring these numbers down? Should they require IDs for all purchases? Put cigarettes behind counters? Prohibit the sale of out-of-package cigarettes (which are more affordable and lack the package's health warnings)? Outlaw cigarette vending machines? Perhaps all of the above? Unfortunately, little was known about the effectiveness of these policies individually or collectively.

Still, states had to act to avoid forfeiting those federal funds. So, in the first year following the passage of the Synar Amendment, ten states immediately began to experiment by passing laws aimed at curbing youth smoking. As Table 1 shows, most of these initial ten states passed a law that mandated a minimum age of 18 to legally purchase cigarettes or a law that banned the sale of cigarettes through vending machines.[34] In addition, a small handful of states tried some other tactics. Connecticut and New York were early leaders in terms of adopting youth access restrictions, followed closely by Florida, Georgia, Oregon, and Vermont, while other states took more of a wait-and-see approach.[35]

Policymakers in other states could observe which types of laws these initial states enacted. In addition, because of the requirement to report yearly rates of both youth smoking and the ability of youths to illegally purchase cigarettes, states were able to see which other states were successful. In short, the conditions

Table 1 Number of states with various youth access restrictions

	1993	*1996*
Set a minimum age for purchase	8	18
Ban on vending machine sales	7	13
Ban on out-of-package sales	4	10
Statewide enforcement office	4	13
Ban on free samples	3	6
Random inspections	2	12
Photo ID required for purchase	2	7
Graduated penalties	2	8
Any type of restriction	*10*	*20*

---

[34] Most of the policies in the table are self-explanatory. Two that require some explanation are statewide enforcement (where states establish new offices to enforce youth access laws and apply penalties) and graduated penalties, which applied both to establishments that sold cigarettes (and ultimately could lose their licenses for repeated violations) and underage smokers.

[35] These observations and data for this section (including Table 1) are drawn from Alciati et al. (1998).

were ripe for learning. By 1996, just three years after the initial experiments, a total of twenty states had adopted new youth smoking laws.

By 2005, every state except Kansas met the federally mandated (below 20 percent youth access) thresholds in their testing programs. Louisiana's youth access rate had fallen to 7.3 percent, reducing its youth access problem to a tenth of its former level. Surveys found falling levels of cigarette use among youths in every state, reaching new lows in many of them by 2005 (dropping to 7 percent in Utah, 25 percent in West Virginia, for example).[36] On the whole, states learned which policies worked elsewhere and copied those that achieved the greatest success.

2.2 Brandeis's Optimism

In 1932, Supreme Court Justice Louis Brandeis observed that "a single courageous State may, if its citizens choose, serve as a laboratory; and try novel social and economic experiments without risk to the rest of the country." In this oft-quoted phrase from his dissenting opinion in the case of *New State Ice Co. v. Liebmann*, Brandeis argued that such experimentation allows us "to remould ... our economic practices and institutions to meet changing social and economic needs." One state chooses to experiment; if the policy succeeds, other states can learn from that experiment and adopt something similar. If the policy fails, others can learn to avoid early pitfalls.

Again, this is the ideal, at least in theory: initial trial and error will lead to the discovery of better policies, which then will diffuse across the states while bad policies are contained. Brandeis essentially was setting out the best-case scenario for policymaking in a federal system.[37] The concept as a whole is worth unpacking. To begin with, a federal system in which states have policymaking authority provides states with the opportunity to experiment with different policies. When an issue like rising rates of youth smoking appears, some states might try requiring IDs for the purchase of cigarettes, others might prohibit cigarette vending machines, and still others might adopt a mixture of different policies.

Next, this system of trial and error at the state level allows for something like a controlled experiment. If Connecticut adopts an ID law, while Oklahoma adopts a law that restricts sales of cigarettes outside of their original packaging, and smoking among teenagers decreases in Connecticut but not Oklahoma, then a plausible inference – assuming all else equal (which is admittedly a big

---

[36] Statistics here are from the 2005 YRBSS survey (www.cdc.gov/mmwr/preview/mmwrhtml/ss5505a1.htm).

[37] For an overview of the potential benefits of federalism, see Bednar 2015.

assumption) – is that ID laws are more effective at reducing smoking than are single-cigarette sales restrictions.[38] In other words, when different experiments are conducted, different outcomes might result, and those outcomes often can be tied back to the experiments. Some experiments will succeed; others will fail.

Both of those aspects – states can experiment and some of those experiments will be more successful than others – are explicit in Brandeis's formulation. A further consideration is more implicit: other states will observe what initial states have done and whether their experiments were successful and then will act on that information. In other words, states will *learn* from these earlier experiments. They will, "without risk," observe the actions taken by other states and the outcomes those actions produced. Then, if they think that one of these earlier policies represents a good option, they can enact that policy themselves. Through this process, policies can spread from one state to the next. More precisely, because a state can observe which policies worked and which did not, good policies will diffuse while bad ones will not.

It is precisely this ideal – good policies will spread, while bad policies will not – that is at the core of Brandeis's optimistic view. But is Brandeis's optimism merited? How likely is it that our federal system, which allows for states to experiment and then for other states to follow their lead, will produce this salutary effect?

2.3 Three Ingredients in the Recipe for Success

We argue that diffusion in a federal system can indeed produce the spread of good policies. As we will show, this normatively appealing outcome is far from certain, but it also is not hopelessly or naively optimistic. The case of youth smoking indicates that Brandeis's optimism was merited, that a federal system can allow for the spread of good, successful policies and the containment of bad ones. Positive outcomes are most likely to occur when states are able to learn from one another, leading to policies that spread through learning, rather than via imitation, competition, or coercion.

What does learning involve? We began to explore this question abstractly in the context of evaluating Brandeis's famous statement about the policymaking benefits of a federal system. Here we delve into it in more detail, identifying the conditions that make learning more likely (although not guaranteed). We distinguish three main ingredients in Brandeis's recipe for success: observable experiments, sufficient time for learning to take place, and policymakers with the proper incentives and expertise. All of these ingredients can be found in the

---

[38] Furthermore, states that adopt a specific combination of approaches might have more success than states that adopt only a single policy.

case of youth smoking policies, which explains why learning was able to occur in this policy area. We first explore these three ingredients in some detail. Then, in Section 2.5, we provide further examples of when these ingredients promoted the diffusion of successful policies.

2.3.1 Observable Experiments

A state that is considering whether or not to adopt a new policy regarding, say, renewable energy policies or fair employment practices, will, as we discussed, consider a mixture of internal and external factors. For US states, these external considerations can derive from a variety of sources – the national government, think tanks, even policies in other countries. However, the policies that other states have adopted are the most prominent and well-documented external sources.

If a state has not yet adopted a policy and is considering adoption, it will look at the actions other states have taken and the experiments they have undertaken.[39] Importantly, when more states have conducted experiments, this provides greater opportunities for the state in question to learn.[40] If, for example, Georgia is trying to figure out which renewable energy policies to enact, and it can draw upon the prior experiences of, say, North Carolina, Colorado, California, and a handful of other states, then it is in a better position to learn about policy effects than if only a single state has acted.[41] To be clear, even if only a single state had adopted a policy, Georgia would still be able to learn from that adoption. That's especially true if the state is viewed as a regional leader possessing great expertise in this policy area, as North Carolina is in the area of renewable energy. But Georgia would be in a better position if multiple states have adopted policies, creating a variety of outcomes from which it could learn. The more experimentation that has occurred, the more opportunities the state has to learn.[42]

However, experimentation on its own is not sufficient. A state that is considering adoption also must be able to see these experiments and determine whether, in its view, the policy choices are good ones. In other words, the experiments must be observable. Sometimes a single high-profile state taking

---

[39] The innovative first-adopting state is also worthy of examination (Parinandi 2020) but is beyond our current focus on policies spreading.

[40] The passage of policies in multiple states facilitates what Rogers (2003, 172–173) calls "information-seeking" and "awareness-knowledge," which are central to learning-based diffusion.

[41] As Parinandi (2020) highlights, states decide which particular sources (e.g., hydroelectric, wind, biomass) to promote, what percentage of electricity provision must come from renewable sources, and so on.

[42] Shipan and Volden (2006, 2008) explore learning about anti-smoking policies across US states and localities.

action is sufficient. North Carolina, as mentioned, is seen as a leader in renewable energy policies, so any actions it takes are likely to be seen by other states. Nevertheless, other factors can influence the likelihood that a state will be able to observe policy experiments.

In the case of youth smoking, states were required to report data on both smoking levels and the rate at which youths were able to illegally purchase cigarettes. The federal government then published these data. Consequently, it was easy for a state to observe which other states were achieving success and then find out what steps – including not just individual policy choices but also combinations of these policies – they had taken. Observability is also promoted through networks of policymakers.[43] The National Conference of State Legislatures, for instance, regularly convenes groups of state legislators and highlights best practices found across the states.

2.3.2 Time to Learn

Learning takes time. States first have to adopt policies. Next the outcomes of those policies need to be observable. Then another state must explore its options to see which ones perform best on key evaluative criteria and to discern which are most appropriate given its own circumstances.

Sometimes states have sufficient time to learn. Other times, however, they do not. The stay-at-home orders issued after COVID-19 broke out in the United States offer an obvious example of a situation in which states basically did not have time to thoroughly and systematically evaluate different options. There is no question that a state might have benefited from the experiences of early adopters. It might have learned whether complete shutdowns were necessary, whether partial shutdowns would be sufficient, and whether any shutdowns should be put in place immediately or only after infections were rising. It might have learned which workers to deem essential. It might have learned whether some locations, such as nursing homes, required extra protections. It might have learned how long the shutdown needed to be in place before states could safely start to reopen their economies. And it might have more accurately determined the trade-offs between health considerations and economic costs. But infections were mounting exponentially and people were dying. States needed to act as soon as possible; time was a luxury they believed they could not afford.

In contrast, because states could observe various youth smoking policies and their effects over multiple years, they were well positioned to identify and adopt good policies. They could also learn after their own initial attempts and

---

[43] Such networks aid learning-based policy diffusion in federal systems worldwide (see, e.g., Füglister 2012 on Switzerland).

improve their policies in light of new information. Furthermore, youth smoking is the type of policy area in which the concept of a good policy or an improvement is much easier to discern.[44] There is widespread agreement that it is good to prevent kids from smoking and to make it harder for them to purchase cigarettes. Benefits from success are felt in both policy outcomes and politics. Even companies that might disagree with laws that aim to limit youth smoking – say, cigarette companies that are looking for long-term customers or stores that would gain a little additional revenue from selling cigarettes to younger people – would be hard pressed to speak out publicly in favor of youth smoking.

Regardless of the criteria used to judge the success of a policy or whether these criteria differ across states, having sufficient time for evaluation is crucial. Policy success often relies on careful implementation and can take months or years to emerge. People must learn about the new policy and change their behavior accordingly. Such behavioral changes may yield policy successes or reveal the policy as ineffectual or even a failure.

2.3.3 Expertise and Incentives

Suppose that both of the other ingredients – observable experiments and time to learn – are in place for a state that is considering the adoption of new policies about the reporting of child abuse. Several other states have adopted policies taking different approaches. The policy details have been collected and disseminated by a foundation that advocates on behalf of children. The state that is trying to decide what policy to enact knows which criteria it wishes to meet to achieve good policy in this area. And it has time to evaluate the different options on these criteria.

Such a state is in a good position to learn, but it needs the *expertise* and *incentives* to do so. State governmental institutions vary tremendously in their ability to acquire and cultivate expertise. For example, some state legislatures have committees that develop expertise in specific policy areas; others do not. Some meet frequently and have the time to discuss different policy options; others do not. Some have extensive staff support; others do not. A minority of states (e.g., Pennsylvania or Michigan) have professional legislatures that pay enough for lawmaking to be a full-time job, whereas legislator pay in the more prevalent citizen legislatures (e.g., Kentucky or Wyoming) is insufficient to fully cultivate lawmaking expertise.

---

[44] Contrast this policy area with, say, the adoption of state lotteries (Berry and Berry 1990), which could be evaluated along multiple dimensions. More generally, see Graham, Shipan, and Volden's (2013, 691) discussion of what constitutes "success" or a "good" policy.

States that build policy expertise with sufficient time to confront multiple policy areas and different policy options, and with dedicated staff to help them develop policies, have a big advantage when it comes to learning. They are more likely to know about experiments that other states have conducted, to be able to evaluate the outcomes of these other experiments, and to figure out which options will work best for them.[45] States that have greater capacities in these areas are better able to learn. For youth smoking, research has revealed that states with greater capacity for developing expertise were more likely to draw on the experiments of successful early adopters.[46]

Beyond expertise, policymakers also must have the proper incentives to learn from others. In highly polarized contexts, policymakers may not even be willing to listen to proposals from those who are ideologically distant or from the opposing political party.[47] Their networks may become constrained, such as when the National Governors Association splintered into the Democratic Governors Association and the Republican Governors Association. And they may be skeptical (perhaps correctly) of evidence from policy entrepreneurs and advocates who have a financial or ideological bias.

Learning from earlier successes is also enhanced when other considerations and incentives are kept at bay. Policies with long-term benefits must not be neglected in favor of short-term electoral concerns. Politicians must be open to meet with and learn from a broad set of individuals, not just lobbyists from organizations that contribute to their campaigns. Policymakers must be more concerned about whether the policies they support will work, rather than how they will be perceived for adopting them. Will they, for example, promote mask-wearing during a pandemic, even if they fear wearing a mask in public makes them look weak? Will they follow the best policy evidence no matter where it leads?

2.4 Combining the Ingredients

Figure 3 displays these three ingredients and shows how they interact. The overlap of Observable Experiments, Time to Learn, and Expertise/Incentives in the middle of the figure offers a clear recipe for the Learning-Based Spread of Good Policies. The omission of any of these essential ingredients can leave a bad taste in policymakers' mouths. As seen in the regions where the circles only partially overlap, without observable experiments from other states, policymakers must rely

---

[45] As Rogers (2003, 173) puts it, they have "principles-knowledge" and "how-to knowledge."

[46] Shipan and Volden (2014) find less evidence of learning within lower-capacity states, such as those with citizen legislatures.

[47] Butler et al. (2017) find that local officials were uninterested in learning about policies from those on the other end of the ideological spectrum, although they were able to overcome this bias through strong evidence of policy success.

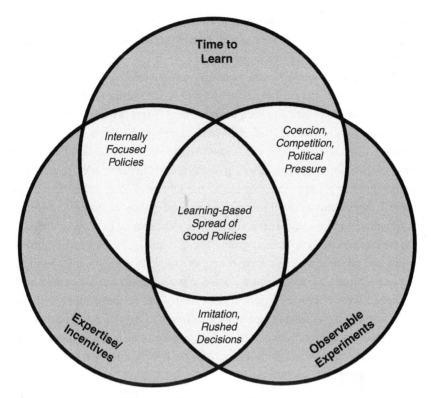

Figure 3 When good policies spread

mainly or even solely upon prior efforts in their own state. They become internally rather than externally focused, yielding no learning from other states and adoptions, which in turn means good policies are less likely to spread across the United States.[48] When such experiments are available, but there is no time to learn, once again the spread of good policies becomes less likely. Decisions are rushed, often based on emerging but as-yet-insufficient evidence. And states are left merely imitating those they hope will succeed rather than those that have demonstrated success. Finally, lacking expertise and the incentives to use that knowledge, states turn away from learning to such other processes as competition and coercion, where they base their decisions on political pressures rather than on the best policy evidence.

But that sweet spot in the middle of the figure, where all the ingredients combine to produce the hoped-for outcome, does exist. States can, and do, learn from one another. In the area of youth smoking, for example, states felt pressure

---

[48] They can, of course, learn from their own internal experiments. This, however, does not facilitate the spread of good policies across states.

to act and to achieve success to avoid substantial financial penalties from the federal government. They were able to learn from the actions of earlier states, which led to the spread of good policies.

Youth smoking thus offers an excellent example of how good policies can spread across the states. However, it is again worth noting all the ingredients that went into this particular recipe for success. There was extensive experimentation in the states, with different states adopting different policies aimed at reducing youth smoking rates and access to cigarettes. The success of each state was compiled and reported, ensuring observability. States needed to act fairly quickly but had enough time to evaluate the actions of other states. There was general agreement on what constituted a good policy outcome and timely information on these key criteria for success. While states in general tended to follow the lead of those demonstrating policy success, the states with greater policy and political expertise were even more likely to draw the right lessons.

In other words, the recipe was followed to perfection in this policy area, with all three of the necessary ingredients present. One concern, though, is that perhaps this is a unique area, one of the few in which everything came together just right. Fortunately, from a normative standpoint, this is not the case. In the next subsection, we highlight a number of other policies in which learning took place and good policies spread.

2.5 Brandeis Was Right (At Least Some of the Time)

In 1996, the Republican Congress and Democratic President Bill Clinton came together to adopt a long-overdue welfare policy reform, replacing the Aid to Families with Dependent Children (AFDC) program with Temporary Assistance for Needy Families (TANF). Among the key components of this change were a shift from a long-term entitlement to "temporary assistance" and a shift from "welfare to work." How long recipients would receive assistance and which programs would support their move into the workforce would be open for state experimentation.

And experiment they did. Across dozens of different components, states tried different policy options. Some put tight limits on how long recipients could stay on the rolls, whereas others were more flexible. Some required just a few hours of work-related activities per week, while others set higher standards. Some counted schoolwork as work-related, whereas others dismissed such efforts. Some offered job training and childcare to help in the transition from welfare to work. And on and on, with no two states' policies being exactly alike.

With only theoretical claims about which of these policies would work, a great experiment was under way, and everyone was watching. Countless think tanks, scholars, and policy analysts assessed the outcomes across important dimensions. How many recipients stayed on the rolls and for how long? How many were successfully placed into jobs? Did reaching the end of the program's time limits yield greater unemployment, greater poverty, greater homelessness?

With all of this evidence available to policymakers, the early years of the TANF program were full of observable experiments, one of the main ingredients for learning and the spread of good policies. As the initial results came in, state policymakers actively modified their programs. States that succeeded on key criteria – rising job placements, reducing the number of recipients, lower poverty – were copied, while failing policies were abandoned.[49] The number of families on the welfare rolls plummeted from around 5 million in the mid-1990s to less than 2 million a decade later, largely due to new employment for recipients.[50] On the whole, the TANF program was seen as wildly successful, especially compared with AFDC, at least until the Great Recession began to put significant strain on the system in 2008.[51]

Drunk driving restrictions provide a second example of the spread of good public policies. Although the first laws against driving while intoxicated were established in New Jersey (in 1906) and New York (in 1910), new restrictions and corresponding penalties were expanded significantly in the 1980s and 1990s, spurred by efforts of organizations such as Mothers Against Drunk Driving (MADD). States experimented with how to best get drivers to change their behavior, trying out different options such as minimum fines, minimum jail time, zero tolerance policies, suspended licenses, and so on.

These policies took a while to succeed, as drivers needed to recognize that states were taking this problem seriously and that they faced serious penalties for their behavior. Over time, however, evidence began to accumulate that states with more comprehensive policies, composed of a mixture of restrictions, monitoring, and enforcement activities, as well as public awareness campaigns, saw greater reductions in alcohol-related fatalities. This evidence was made clear to state legislators, especially in areas with a greater MADD presence, and states modified their policies as a result. It was not so much that states that previously had ignored drunk driving now acted. Rather, states revisited and

---

[49] Volden (2016) shows that policy successes were adopted but failures were abandoned and avoided by others. Consistent with the need for expertise, these findings were stronger among states with more professional legislatures.

[50] Data are available at https://aspe.hhs.gov/report/welfare-indicators-and-risk-factors-thirteenth-report-congress/afdctanf-program-data.

[51] See Schram and Soss (2001) for early concerns.

reinvented their existing policies, making them more comprehensive.[52] Comprising more than 40 percent of all traffic-related deaths in the United States in the mid-1980s, alcohol-related deaths now constitute less than 30 percent of all traffic fatalities.[53]

Yet another example of the learning-based spread of good policies comes in the area of children's health insurance. In 1997, Congress established the state Children's Health Insurance Program (CHIP), offering states generous grants to extend health insurance benefits to families who otherwise could not afford them (but who earned too much to be eligible for Medicaid). The grants were so attractive that all states adopted a CHIP program within its first year in existence. Yet these programs varied substantially in their eligibility and benefit levels, in whether they included monthly premiums and copayments for doctor visits, and in their waiting periods for enrollment, among other considerations.

As with all new policies, some worked better than others at lowering the rates of uninsured poor children in the states. As officials sought information about what other states were doing, they quickly established a network of experts. Through "CHIP CHAT," emails were immediately shared across all state CHIP administrators. They discussed how their programs were to be implemented, concerns they had about these programs, new ideas they were considering, and what worked well. Based on these expert conversations, state health officials and legislatures modified their programs more than 100 times over the first four years of the program's existence. They abandoned elements that were not working and adopted those found in successful states.[54] Importantly, the incentives were right for doing so. Democrats and Republicans alike sought to take credit for the highly popular program. State legislators who were concerned about the program's cost were won over by the significant grants from the federal government that offset those expenses to a large degree. Within its first few years, the program succeeded in lifting more than 6 million children from the ranks of the uninsured.

These policy successes in areas as diverse as welfare, drunk driving, and health insurance show that the youth smoking example was not unique. They also demonstrate that the same three ingredients were at work in the learning-based spread of each of these good policies. The TANF program was full of observable experiments that other states could learn from. Drunk driving

---

[52] Yu, Jennings, and Butler (2020) document the comprehensiveness of state drunk driving policies, showing how they changed in response to the emerging evidence of policy success, and how this evidence was bolstered by MADD lobbying efforts. For more on policy reinvention, see Glick and Hayes (1991).

[53] Data are from www.iii.org/fact-statistic/facts-statistics-alcohol-impaired-driving.

[54] Volden (2006) demonstrates that the most successful states served as sources for others in modifying their CHIP programs during the initial years of the program.

policies took time to work, but that time was used to draw clear lessons that more comprehensive policies were more effective. In the CHIP program, expertise was quickly developed through networks such as CHIP CHAT, and incentives were aligned for success through intergovernmental grants.

On the whole, the promise of American federalism as put forward by Brandeis seems to be a dream realized in multiple policy areas. With such successes, one is left to wonder: what could possibly go wrong?

3 What Could Possibly Go Wrong?

3.1 Three Strikes against State Criminal Justice Policymaking

One vast area of state policymaking involves criminal justice. From the death penalty to concealed carry gun laws, from hate crimes to combatting organized crime, states play a major policy role. Could the adoption of these policies provide further examples of the learning-based spread of good policies, similar to what we saw with drunk driving laws in Section 2? Yes. However, many things could go wrong as states attempt to navigate this complicated policy area.

The example of criminal sentencing guidelines illustrates some potential pitfalls. For starters, deciding which sentences are appropriate upon conviction of a crime is a complex matter. The nature of the crime certainly should factor into that calculation, but mitigating and aggravating circumstances surrounding the crime also present relevant information. Considerations about the criminal's past behaviors and likely recidivism upon release also matter. Moreover, the severity of sentences may deter future crime.

Lacking particular expertise in matters of criminal justice, state lawmakers long avoided establishing specific sentencing guidelines, instead opting for systems of "indeterminate sentencing." In such a system, states would set maximum sentences – often quite high – for various crimes. Judges, working with prosecutors, would have discretion to set prison terms, such as five-to-ten years. Parole boards would determine whether prisoners within that time frame were fit to be released into society.

Over time, concerns grew about the efficacy of this system. To many, it appeared arbitrary, with large disparities in time served by offenders who committed essentially the same crime. Tough-on-crime critics pointed to cases in which a convict was released after limited jail time and then quickly committed another offense. Victims' rights groups argued that victims of crimes often were surprised by the early release of violent offenders. Others raised concerns about biases in the system, including longer sentences for members of racial minority groups than for white people who committed the same crime.

Beginning in the 1970s, states began to consider "determinate sentencing" policies – sentences of specific length that cannot be changed – which significantly limited the discretion of judges and parole boards. In 1980, the Minnesota state legislature became the first to adopt such sentencing guidelines. Over the next decade, a dozen other states followed suit, while Congress adopted sentencing guidelines for federal crimes in the Comprehensive Crime Control Act of 1984.[55]

Factors internal to states certainly influenced the adoption of sentencing guidelines (e.g., states with higher violent crime rates were more likely to adopt stricter guidelines). But external factors of policy diffusion also mattered.[56] Had this diffusion process been based primarily on learning about policy successes, the spread would have taken a long time. Judges would have to change their behavior, criminals would have to serve their time, and analysts would need to explore both the effects of these changes on subsequent recidivism and whether there were biases in how different types of defendants were treated. Information would then eventually spread across states.

Instead, for many states and the federal government, public pressure meant that they had insufficient time to generate and share such information. Rather than learning, they engaged in a process of imitation, copying popular policies prior to the availability of evidence of success. In other cases, the learning process was short-circuited by political biases. Evidence strongly suggests that the spread of sentencing guidelines was based more on ideological leanings than on learning.[57]

Such political considerations in this first wave of sentencing guidelines presaged additional state involvement in criminal justice sentencing. Following guidelines from the 1984 federal law, many states adopted "mandatory minimum" sentences, further limiting judicial discretion. A decade later, Congress passed the Violent Crime Control and Law Enforcement Act of 1994. Coerced by federal grants in this law, states quickly adopted "truth in sentencing" laws, whereby prisoners would serve the entirety of their sentences without the possibility of early parole.[58] Eleven states adopted such laws in the first year of the program, with more than half of all states doing so by 1998. Throughout the 1990s, many states also adopted "three strikes" laws – which we discuss in Section 3.3.3 – whereby sentences are significantly increased (often

---

[55] See Shepherd (2002) and Stemen and Rengifo (2011) for information on determinate sentencing policies and their effects.

[56] Diffusion studies that explore the spread of criminal sentencing policies include Boushey (2010) and Karch et al. (2016).

[57] For evidence of the ideological underpinnings in the adoption of sentencing guidelines, see Grossback, Nicholson-Crotty, and Peterson (2004).

[58] Details on the adoption of these laws can be found at https://bjs.gov/content/pub/pdf/tssp.pdf.

to life in prison without the possibility of parole) for those previously convicted of two serious crimes.[59] The most highly publicized and widely criticized version of this law was passed directly by California voters in a proposition measure in 1994.

On its face, one might expect problems to arise when a complex area like criminal justice law is boiled down to a baseball analogy and taken out of the hands of expert judges, prosecutors, and parole boards, to be set instead by voters or generalists in the state legislatures.[60] Tough-on-crime positions are politically popular, often even in the face of falling crime rates.[61] But is it fair to label such widespread policies as "bad"? There is substantial variation in state policies and their effects, along with significant evidence that these laws on the whole have reduced crime and recidivism. Indeed, if a prisoner is never released, there is no opportunity for further crimes. Such benefits, however, must be weighed against the costs. Comparisons across countries may also be helpful in reaching such judgments. For example, even though violent crime rates are approximately the same in Europe and the United States, per capita incarceration rates in the United States are nearly ten times those found in Europe.[62]

Moreover, arguments in favor of using sentencing guidelines to remove racial and other biases seem to ring hollow in light of such biases continuing (and perhaps increasing) in the presence of sentencing guidelines. Today, incarceration rates are five times greater among African Americans and twice as great among Latinos as among white Americans. One stark comparison noted that "there are more African American men incarcerated in the U.S. than the total prison populations in India, Argentina, Canada, Lebanon, Japan, Germany, Finland, Israel and England combined."[63] Critics point to numerous examples of how such biases arose from minimum sentencing laws, such as the harsher sentencing guidelines for crack cocaine use (affecting minority communities) than for powder cocaine (more common among affluent whites). Such racial disparities in turn affect family structures, employment opportunities, cycles of poverty, policing practices, and numerous other policies that perpetuate racial inequalities throughout the United States today.

The example of criminal justice policies illustrates many of the possibilities for what could go wrong on the path to the learning-based spread of good policies. Rather than taking time to learn, states rushed to appear tough on

---

[59] Karch and Cravens (2014) study the diffusion of three strikes laws across the states.

[60] Fay and Wenger (2016) explore how different constitutional hurdles for policy change across the states affect the rate and nature of diffusion.

[61] Enns (2014) explores the effect of public opinion on tough-on-crime policies.

[62] See www.nationmaster.com/country-info/compare/European-Union/United-States/Crime.

[63] This quote and surrounding statistics come from www.huffpost.com/entry/black-mass-incarceration-statistics_b_6682564.

crime. Rather than relying on experts, voters and policy generalists instead played a major role. And rather than thoughtful learning, states imitated the toughest policies they could find. In sum, much could – and did – go wrong.

3.2 "Might Happen" Does Not Mean "Will Happen"

Sections 1 and 2 establish that good policies can spread when states learn from one another. To repeat the factors supporting the diffusion of good policies: some initial states experiment; some of those experiments succeed; policy-makers in other states observe those experiments; they have time to evaluate which experiments were successful; and they have the expertise and incentives to determine which ones are appropriate for their own states. When the process plays out this way, bad policies are weeded out while good policies survive, spread, and thrive. Justice Brandeis then can rest happily, knowing that his optimism about states serving as effective policy laboratories was merited.

Nevertheless, a lot has to line up just right for this positive outcome to transpire. If a policy runs into problems at any of these steps – if, for example, states do not notice the results of early experiments or if they lack the expertise to understand these experiments – then we might not attain the positive outcomes promised by a federal system. Something has gone wrong.

In this section, we have two primary goals. Our first goal is to explore why learning might not take place and why, as a result, states might not adopt good policies. The characteristics of policies and issues themselves provide one potential obstacle to the spread of good policies. When these characteristics impede learning, they can hinder the spread of good policies. Biases that are inherent in policymaking, such as short time horizons and a tendency to rely on easily available information, provide a second set of obstacles. A final set of obstacles arises when politicians, along with the institutions that surround them, lack sufficient expertise or capabilities to learn and to adopt good policies.

Our second goal is to understand why states might adopt bad policies. To this end, in Section 3.6 we focus on diffusion mechanisms other than learning and assess the implications of these mechanisms for policy adoptions. Although learning is desirable, it is neither automatic nor guaranteed and, consequently, might not occur. In the absence of learning, diffusion is driven by competition, imitation, and coercion, all of which can make the spread of bad policies more likely.

3.3 Some Policies Promote Learning More Than Others Do

Scholars of policy diffusion have highlighted six attributes of policies themselves that influence whether and how they spread across the states, and thus whether learning is likely.[64] For two of these attributes – observability and relative advantage – their *absence* will inhibit the learning-based spread of good policies. For two others – complexity and incompatibility – their *presence* can undermine learning. The final two attributes – salience and trialability – yield mixed implications.

3.3.1 Observability and Relative Advantage

In Figure 3 we identified observability (Observable Experiments) as one of the main ingredients for learning. Here we need add only that observability can be a function of specific policies, where some policies (and their effects) are easily observed, but others are not. For example, few people will know about a state's witness intimidation laws or how effective they are until some rare crisis arises. In general, policies that are more observable both in their adoption and in their effectiveness are more likely to spread.[65]

Relative advantage is defined as the degree to which a new policy outperforms the old policy, featuring lower costs, higher benefits, or both. The relative advantage of a policy is linked to its success or how good the policy is, but it takes that assessment a step further. Rather than evaluating a policy in and of itself, relative advantage compares that policy to the state's current status quo policy. A new policy to regulate fishing in Alaska, for example, may have long-term sustainability benefits that exceed short-term costs. But if the current policy is already working well, perhaps with even more sustainable fishing yields at lower costs, the new policy may actually lack a relative advantage. In contrast, if Illinois is struggling with rules regarding corruption, a new policy with benefits even somewhat exceeding costs may present a substantial relative advantage. A successful policy, in other words, is more likely to diffuse when it offers a relative advantage over existing policies.

3.3.2 Complexity and Incompatibility

In contrast to observability and relative advantage, the *presence* of complexity and incompatibility can create substantial obstacles to policy learning and the spread of good policies. Complexity refers to the degree to which the

---

[64] Rogers (2003) discusses these attributes and their influence on the diffusion of all sorts of innovations, not just in the policy realm. Nicholson-Crotty (2009) explores the role of salience and complexity in policy diffusion. Makse and Volden (2011) introduce the other attributes to the policy diffusion literature, showing how they influence both geographic and learning-based diffusion. These studies undergird our discussion throughout this subsection.

[65] Conversely, observable failures are less likely to spread. Volden (2016) studies the abandonment of policy failures in the context of welfare reforms. Mooney (2001) discusses similar concerns surrounding regional policy diffusion.

assessment and implementation of a policy require specialized knowledge and technical expertise.[66] Of course, every policy, even a simple one, contains some complexity. Consider the adoption of seat belt laws in the states. The main question states faced was: Should seat belts be required? Yet, once a state decides that the answer to this question is "yes," it still needs to address a host of other issues. Should only drivers be required to wear seat belts or should passengers, too? Should all children be required to wear seat belts or should there be exemptions (or additional requirements) based on age, height, or weight? What should be done about older cars that do not have seat belts installed in them? Should trucks be treated the same as cars?

Some of these questions are fairly easy to address. But others are more complex[67], especially when they require technical knowledge. For example, computer simulations and crash tests might provide relevant information about the ways in which seat belts can be made safer for children, as might observational data based on actual crashes. Such tests require at least some technical expertise to assess them. Still, the level of technical expertise needed to make law in this area pales in comparison with, say, energy or environmental policies, which require advanced knowledge of engineering, physics, and chemistry; health policies, which require medical and scientific expertise; or banking regulations, which require specialized expertise in economics and law.[68]

The effect of complexity on the diffusion of good policies is relatively straightforward and connects with our expertise condition. A complex policy may be a good one; however, for it to spread, other states will need a heightened ability to evaluate it. States that lack expertise often have insufficient capacity to learn about complex policies (as we discuss further in Section 3.5.1). Even if it has limited expertise, a state may be able to learn fairly quickly about simple policies, like seat belt laws or how much to charge for admission to state parks. The situation is different, though, if a state is trying to fight a pandemic caused by a novel virus.

Complex policies also have been shown to take longer to diffuse. If a policy is complex, and a state faces even moderate time pressures, it might not be able to learn about that policy. Thus, a complex policy is less likely to diffuse to other states than a simpler policy, even if the complex policy is a good one. In one

---

[66] See Rogers (2003) and Nicholson-Crotty (2009) for the role that complexity plays in state policymaking and diffusion.

[67] Legislatures regularly delegate even straightforward policies to agencies to deal with hidden complexities (Clouser McCann and Shipan forthcoming), which can increase the amount of time needed for learning to take place.

[68] Nicholson-Crotty (2009) categorizes energy, environmental, health, taxation, trade, and fiscal regulation policies as complex, and criminal justice, education, morality, civil rights, consumer protection, and electoral policies as less complex.

study of dozens of criminal justice policies, for example, states were twice as likely to adopt policies judged to be low in complexity as they were to adopt highly complex policies in any given year.[69]

The compatibility of a policy – that is, its fit with the current policies, needs, and characteristics of a particular state – also influences its spread. A state like Ohio might develop a set of urban renewal policies that work well in a rust belt city like Cleveland that is trying to reinvent itself. If that policy succeeds, it might find a receptive audience in Michigan (with Detroit), Pennsylvania (with Pittsburgh), Wisconsin (with Milwaukee), and Missouri (with St. Louis). While these states might learn from Ohio's experiment, other states that lack major urban areas, like Vermont, North Dakota, or Wyoming, or states with different kinds of cities, such as Arizona, North Carolina, or Utah, might find little to learn from Ohio's urban renewal experiments.[70]

Highly compatible policies often represent small changes to the status quo. To fit well with existing policies and practices, major changes are set aside in favor of incremental steps. As such, compatible policies often lack the benefits that would arise from a more global search.[71] On the flip side, states are unlikely to adopt incompatible policies, which are policies that represent a substantial change from the way states have always done things. Two states whose prior policies have not converged may therefore face great difficulty in learning from each other. A small and compatible policy shift in one state may look like an enormous and incompatible change elsewhere.[72] Mail-in voting during a pandemic, for example, may be a compatible policy for states that already have extensive absentee voting allowances, such as Hawaii or New Mexico, but may be incompatible and tougher to implement in states that have relied mainly or solely on in-person voting, such as Kentucky or Tennessee.

3.3.3 Salience and Trialability

Although in some ways linked to observability, the traits of salience and trialability produce more mixed effects on the possibility of learning. Salience can draw the attention of policymakers to an issue, giving them an incentive to address it. Policymakers in a state where crime rates are low and perhaps more

---

[69] See Makse and Volden (2011).

[70] Examples of policy compatibility concerns abound. For example, speed limit laws that make sense in a densely populated state like New Jersey might be pointless in Montana. Daylight saving time laws might promise numerous benefits to more urban and tourism-based states like Florida, while having more negative effects on farm- and agriculture-based states like Nebraska.

[71] See Kollman, Miller, and Page (2000), Callander (2011), and Glick (2012) regarding the benefits and costs of searching broadly for new policy solutions.

[72] Nicholson-Crotty and Carley (2016) explore compatibility in terms of the implementation of renewable portfolio standard environmental policies.

importantly where citizens perceive that crime rates are low might feel less need to search for policies that will reduce gang violence. On the other hand, if policymakers believe that gangs are becoming more active and their constituents regularly raise concerns about crime, then they are more likely to look for policies that address this issue.[73]

However, although salience draws leaders' attention to an issue, this does not necessarily imply that they will *learn* about existing policies elsewhere. Consider restrictions on smoking in restaurants and bars that states enacted during the 1990s and 2000s. A standard learning-based diffusion view would hold that policymakers in one state observe and adopt good policies from other states. However, public attention to salient policies can place limits on our "Time to Learn" condition. Put simply, people in neighboring states may observe the policy change elsewhere and demand similar and immediate action at home. Such "social contagion" seemed to be behind the spread of many anti-smoking policy adoptions.[74] Demand for policy change may arise because of action on a highly salient policy elsewhere, regardless of whether or not the policy is successful.[75] What is learned is that another state acted, but perhaps not whether its policies were good.

Salient policies also spread faster.[76] When the public is paying attention, political leaders have a greater incentive to move quickly. Interestingly, the effects of complexity and salience can combine. Highly complex policies of low salience spread most slowly, while those that are highly salient but simple spread most quickly. The latter is exemplified by three strikes laws, which, as noted earlier, were based on a simple policy idea – mandatory life sentences for a third major criminal conviction. They were also highly salient, attracting the attention (and often support) of the public. Once the state of Washington first adopted this policy, twenty-four other states followed suit within just two years.

Finally, trialability is the degree to which a policy may be tried and abandoned at a low cost, both politically and in terms of its implementation. On the one hand, trialability may be naturally linked to policy experimentation and the learning that goes with it. If it is too costly to switch to a new policy, few states will experiment. Green energy policies, for example, require a long-term commitment to nurturing new industries and infrastructures and might be highly

---

[73] As Eshbaugh-Soha (2006, 227) explains, salience "demands that elected representatives respond to the public or face electoral consequences or a decline in public support."

[74] See Pacheco (2012).

[75] Pacheco and Maltby (2017) find a similar pattern in the state adoption of policy choices regarding the Affordable Care Act.

[76] See Karch (2007), Nicholson-Crotty (2009), Boushey (2010), and Mallinson (2016).

disruptive of current behaviors. Many states are hesitant to take significant steps in these directions, since reversing course if they fail could be extremely costly.

On the other hand, if it is easy to try a new policy on a temporary basis, that too may undermine learning. Why should policymakers work hard to observe how well a policy performs elsewhere and to adapt those policies to their own circumstances when they could just give it a go themselves? In the criminal justice area, researchers found no learning-based policy diffusion for policies that were easily tried, like Amber Alerts (emergency messages authorities send to notify the public that a child has been abducted) or prisoner furloughs, whereas learning was more likely with policies that were less trialable but easier to observe.[77]

3.4 Biased Policymaking May Limit Learning

Section 3.3 identifies the ways in which attributes of policies themselves can limit the ability of states to learn about and pass good policies. But it is not just policy attributes that can get in the way of good policies spreading. So can politics. Here we focus on three crucial ways in which politics – including the incentives and biases of politicians – can impede the spread of good policies. First, politicians often engage in short-term thinking and short-sighted policy-making. Second, they face incentives to pander to voters and cater to wealthy donors. And, third, they rely on cognitive shortcuts when evaluating policy options.

3.4.1 Short-Term Thinking

As we discussed, many politicians turn to public service because they want to influence public policy, especially in a few areas that are of special interest to them. But even newly elected officials know that their next election is right around the corner. Every two or four years, state legislators and governors experience another round of elections, which means that electoral politics is always on their minds. Although having time to learn is essential, time is always in short supply. The term limits found in many states may add even more urgency to the mix.

The immediate presence of elections can help ensure that the actions of legislators and governors do not stray too far from what citizens in their districts and states prefer. But it also has a downside, in that state-level politicians have

---

[77] Makse and Volden (2011) used expert surveys to rate twenty-seven criminal justice policies in terms of their policy attributes and then explored their diffusion across states. While trialability limited learning, highly observable policies doubled the probability of learning, and highly complex policies cut learning in half.

little incentive to take a long-term view of policy. Instead, they may turn to quick fixes that are not as carefully crafted as they should be, that may not fit in their states, and that might not produce good long-term outcomes. After a long winter that has damaged state highways, for example, politicians who face intense pressure from constituents to fix cracks and potholes are much less likely to take a long-term view about road repairs. Instead, they know that their constituents want something done, and they want it done now. Rather than spending the time to learn about longer-term and potentially better solutions, such politicians are much more likely to support a quick fix, patching potholes time and again.

Elections affect the diffusion of policies with short-term costs and long-term benefits. Needed tax increases are pushed off until after the next election.[78] Policies to address long-term environmental issues, such as greenhouse gases and climate change, present such significant short-term costs that state policy-makers may prefer to ignore them, even when the next election is years away.

3.4.2 Pandering to Voters, Catering to Special Interests

The frequency of elections is thus one source of problems, since it creates pressure to act quickly and implement short-term fixes, both of which run counter to the requirement that learning takes time. An additional election-related pressure is the need to cater to the individuals and groups that will be most helpful for reelection. Of course, this also raises the appealing prospect of politicians being attentive to their constituents. But it can produce biases – specifically, pandering to voters and catering to special interests – that under-mine learning and the spread of good policies.

In particular, politicians might lean toward policies that make for good politics, rather than those that make for good policy. Good politics and good policy can align but do not always do so. Two policies from the area of public health and welfare illustrate this dynamic. One concerns needle exchange programs. Prior to the outbreak of AIDS in the United States in 1981, most states had laws that made it illegal to possess or distribute needles for the purpose of using illegal drugs. With the AIDS outbreak, though, public health experts quickly realized that the provision of clean needles (which would discourage the reuse and sharing of needles) was cost effective and improved overall public health outcomes.[79] Although some states adopted needle exchange programs, many did not, in part because politicians were leery of

---

[78] Berry and Berry (1992) show that proximity to the next election is a factor limiting the adoption of tax increases.

[79] See Bramson et al. (2015) for a discussion of these policies and their effectiveness.

supporting a program that promised benefits to a group of people – drug users – who were held in low esteem by the public.

A second example comes from the area of homelessness. Broadly speaking, subnational governments in the United States have adopted two very different approaches to this issue: criminalization of visible homelessness versus treating it as a public health problem. The cities of Anchorage (Alaska) and Jackson (Michigan) fall into the former category, by relying mainly on policing. Meanwhile, Denver (Colorado) and Boston (Massachusetts), along with the states of North Carolina and California, have taken public health approaches to this issue. Overall, despite strong evidence supporting the success of various public health approaches, criminalization made better politics in many states by targeting a population viewed unfavorably by voters.[80]

Another bias that pushes toward good politics rather than good policies has to do with *which* interests are best represented in policymaking. The concept of "pluralism" suggests that when all interests are represented, the outcome will be good public policy. The problem, however, is one that Schattschneider (1960, pp. 34–35) captured long ago with perhaps the most evocative sentence ever written about policymaking in the United States: "The flaw in the pluralist heaven is that the heavenly chorus sings with a strong upper-class accent." Although good policies stand a fair chance of being selected if all groups are equally represented, in reality the middle class and (especially) the poor are significantly underrepresented.

Policymakers are more likely to meet with campaign contributors than other constituents.[81] That is just good (electoral) politics, but this tendency can result in biased policymaking. Across numerous policy areas, strong evidence shows that economic elites and business interest groups have more influence on policy selection than do average voters.[82] To be clear, these sorts of findings do not rule out the possibility that good policies might spread. But they do indicate that good politics – catering to bigger and wealthier groups – can play a dominant role in policymaking.

Put simply, Figure 3 emphasized the importance of policymakers having the right incentives to learn about good policy. If, instead, they are more interested in learning about whether a policy is good or bad *politically*, policy successes may yield to political successes. At an extreme level, politicians may dismiss evidence-based learning altogether. It may be easier to ignore inconvenient truths, label them as "fake news," or spin them in a more favorable direction.

---

[80] See Willison (2021).
[81] See Miler (2010).
[82] See Gilens and Page (2014) for evidence from nearly 2,000 policy issues.

Both the evidence that reaches policymakers and what they do with that evidence are of major importance.

3.4.3 Availability and Representativeness Biases

Further biases in the way policymakers approach learning from other states arise because of how difficult learning truly is, even when policymakers have the right incentives to engage in learning. The most robust learning from the policy experiments of others involves weighing the evidence of all the costs and all the benefits of all the policies found in all the other states. In reality, however, cognitive limitations (which characterize human decision-making generally) interfere with such policy learning in fundamental ways.[83] For example, when policymakers hunt for good, new policies, they typically do not conduct a systematic search for the best policy. Instead, they satisfice – that is, satisfy themselves with something that suffices – rather than optimize.[84] Due to time limitations and cognitive limitations, they search until they find what appears to be a "good enough" outcome and then adopt that policy. This does not mean that policies that spread will be bad ones – indeed, they very well could be good. However, it means that better policy options often will not even be considered, because the policy search has been called off.

One prominent shortcut that limits learning-based policy diffusion is the *availability* heuristic.[85] Rather than conducting a wide and unlimited search for the best options, people tend to rely on and be most influenced by those options that are readily available to them – options that tend to be more noticeable, salient, and close at hand. In the past, this has meant that the spread of policies was geographically limited. More recently, given how polarized American politics has become, availability is more tightly linked to political ideology.[86] A broader or more fully rational search would undoubtedly uncover other, perhaps better, alternatives, but policymakers turn to readily available options. Policymakers in Indiana who are considering the adoption of new gun control measures could conduct a full search of policies from around the country. Instead, they are likely to be especially

---

[83] Weyland (2007) shows how rational learning gives way to heuristics and shortcuts in policy diffusion. Tversky and Kahneman (1973, 1974) demonstrate how common such heuristics are in human thinking and resulting decisions, while Kahneman (2011) highlights the connection between these biases and "thinking fast or slow."

[84] See Simon (1947) for details of satisficing processes.

[85] Lau and Redlawsk (2001) demonstrate that individuals rely more heavily on heuristics when the policymaking environment is complex.

[86] Mallinson (2021) shows the movement from geographic policy diffusion to polarized ideological diffusion, on average, across 556 policies.

influenced by recent, high-profile debates about and adoptions of policies in their neighboring states of Illinois and Ohio or in other states with similar ideological leanings. In so doing, they may be missing policies that are better at reducing gun violence, are based on more thorough expert analysis, and so on.

Joining the availability heuristic is the *representativeness* heuristic, which causes people to "draw excessively clear, confident, and firm inferences from a precarious base of data."[87] In terms of policy diffusion, this heuristic leads to the quickly acquired belief that one state's success with a policy is representative of what will happen elsewhere. It results, once again, in limiting a search for good policies upon finding one example that is seemingly representative of all other experiences, leading policymakers to generalize from a few examples. Policymakers in South Carolina, for example, might have observed that although New York was among the first states to enact a mask-wearing mandate, COVID-19 cases continued to grow even after the mandate was put in place. Assuming a similar pattern would hold over time and elsewhere, they might then conclude that mask mandates do not work.[88]

In sum, policymakers face many biases that limit their ability to learn about good policies elsewhere and to adopt them at home. They have unduly short time horizons. They pander to voters' whims. They cater to campaign contributors and special interests. They examine policies based on their availability. They consider limited examples as overly representative. These five biases present tremendous challenges to the learning-based spread of good policies, but they also present opportunities for improving public policymaking in ways that we will explore in detail in Section 4.

3.5 Political Institutions Can Undermine Learning

In addition to considering individual-level biases, it is also important to think about the broader political institutions within which policymakers operate. The nature of those institutions often determines the abilities of and incentives for policymakers to engage in learning-based policy diffusion. In this section, we pay particular attention to the expertise and incentives of state legislators, who often play a central role in developing state-level policies.[89]

---

[87] See Weyland (2005, 284).

[88] Bricker and LaCombe (2021) show how states perceived to be similar are more likely to serve as sources of policy ideas, regardless of whether those perceptions match reality.

[89] In focusing on state legislators, we set aside an in-depth consideration of some of the incentives and abilities of other political actors, whether they be governors, voters, or others. That said, where these actors play significant roles in the spread of good (or bad) public policies, we include them among our examples.

3.5.1 Insufficient Expertise to Learn

State legislatures vary considerably in their organization and in the opportunities they offer legislators to learn about and enact good policies. First and foremost, they vary in their capacity to develop expertise. With this capacity, legislatures can hold their own against governors, even when their preferences conflict.[90] But those who lack expertise often must resort to broadly delegating policymaking decisions to executive agencies, where expertise is more plentiful and where the policy is at greater risk of being bent to the will of the governor.

Capacity and expertise also influence whether legislators can learn from other states. One organizational component that influences capacity is legislative committees – their existence, their structure, and the role they play in the legislature. Legislative committees can perform several functions simultaneously.[91] For example, they allow members to direct benefits to their constituents, and they help political parties achieve their goals. Crucially, however, they also provide a forum for the development of expertise, since members who serve on the committee tend to become specialists on topics in the committee's jurisdiction.

If a legislature has a committee dedicated entirely to agricultural issues, as does the Mississippi legislature, it is far more likely to develop expertise on agriculture among the committee's members and for the legislature as a whole than would a legislature lacking an agriculture committee. State legislatures vary considerably in the number of committees they maintain, the jurisdictions of those committees, and the degree to which lawmaking is conducted within committees as opposed to on the floor or via closed-door partisan deal making. Expertise generated in committees in turn allows the legislature to learn about and evaluate policy experiments in other states.

Having more staff also increases legislative capacity. All legislatures rely on some legislative staff, of course. But when individual legislators have their own staff dedicated to policymaking, they can direct these staff members to focus on specific areas and develop expertise.[92] Similarly, legislatures that hire more committee staff are better able to develop the expertise that a committee can provide.

3.5.2 Not Enough Time or Money

Two other factors can affect the development of expertise. First, some legislatures pay fairly well, while others do not. California tops the list, paying

---

[90] Huber and Shipan (2002) explain how legislative capacity and institutional policymaking capacity affect the legislature's ability to constrain the executive branch.

[91] See Maltzman (1998). Gilligan and Krehbiel (1990) detail the informational and expertise benefits of committees.

[92] Bucchianeri, Volden, and Wiseman (2020) show that states with personal staff empower rank-and-file members to be more effective lawmakers.

members more than $100,000 per year (plus a per diem of nearly $200 for each day in session). Other states, such as Pennsylvania and New York, are not far behind. At the other end of the spectrum, New Mexico pays its legislators no yearly salary (with a per diem of $160), and New Hampshire pays only $200 for a two-year term, with no per diem.[93] Higher-paying legislatures induce a different mix of candidates, representing a broader segment of society and attracting those who consider policymaking to be a profession.[94]

State legislatures also vary substantially in how frequently they meet. The Texas and Idaho legislatures meet for only a few months every other year. Meanwhile, other legislatures, like those in Michigan and California, are almost always in session. When a legislature meets for only a limited time, it will have less ability to engage in activities that facilitate learning about policies enacted elsewhere. Instead, it will spend most of its time dealing with essential internal issues, like passing the state budget.

In combination, these factors – the presence of expert committees and staff members, salary and the nature of who runs for office, and how frequently a legislature meets – collectively characterize the degree of professionalism of the state legislature.[95] Less professional legislatures tend to lack the expertise necessary to observe, consider, and assess policy experiments conducted by other states. This in turn decreases the likelihood that they will engage in the learning needed to help good policies spread to their states. Some states may prefer to have "citizen legislatures," such as in the large New Hampshire House of Representatives, where service is viewed not as a profession but rather something that average citizens should take turns doing. But this approach comes at the cost of being less able to learn about good policies found in other states. To be clear, states with low legislative capacity for developing expertise still can learn from other places. They are just less likely to be able to do so than states with greater professionalism, capacity, and expertise.

The issue of youth smoking policies provides a useful example. Recall that we described how learning led to the diffusion of policies designed to reduce youth access to tobacco. States conducted experiments that were highly visible in terms of both their implementation and their effects. This meant that policy-makers who were still considering which policies to enact could see which states had successfully brought down youth smoking rates, as well as the specific policies those states had enacted. States were more likely to enact the

---

[93] www.ncsl.org/research/about-state-legislatures/legislator-compensation-2018.aspx

[94] Hall (2019) shows how salaries influence who seeks to become a state legislator. Diversity of perspectives can be valuable in achieving better decision-making (Page 2008).

[95] Squire (2007) offers an index of state legislative professionalism based on salaries, staff, and time in session.

combination of policies found in successful states than those found in less successful states.[96] But there was also significant variation across the states. State legislatures with high levels of capacity were about three times more likely than those that were below average to learn from earlier experiments and adopt successful ones.

3.5.3 Lacking Facilitators for Policy Learning

The previous subsections have focused on the biases and capacities of policymakers themselves. Yet, other participants in the policymaking process also influence whether states learn from one another. Although these participants can be categorized in various ways – from interest groups to the media to entrepreneurs – here we place them under the umbrella term of "facilitators," to capture the idea that their presence can facilitate the spread of good policies, while their absence can hinder this spread.

An example from environmental policymaking illustrates how organizations can act as facilitators. Although many environmental issues are high profile, others are not. For example, despite the enormous environmental effects of buildings – which consume large amounts of electricity, energy, and water and produce air pollutants at high rates – public officials generally paid little attention to how "green" buildings were until the 1990s.[97] This changed when "environmental knowledge brokers" began to play a substantial facilitator role by establishing the US Green Building Council (USGBC) in 1993. Consisting of public officials, community advocates, and professionals like architects and developers, the USGBC set green standards for new buildings. To support its efforts, the organization strategically established both a national presence and eighty local chapters, which pushed state and local officials to adopt their recommended standards. They achieved remarkable success in an otherwise low-salience policy area, with their recommendations spreading widely across the country.

Organizations like the USGBC often have a clear agenda they are trying to promote. Some focus on a specific policy issue, like green buildings. For others, the agenda is broader – the conservative American Legislative Exchange Council (ALEC) widely disseminates model legislation on topics including workers' rights, tort reform, guns, and immigration.[98] Their goal is to reduce

---

[96] See Shipan and Volden (2014).

[97] For details, see Koski (2010).

[98] Some model laws are adapted from those that currently exist in a state; in other cases, ALEC drafts them from scratch. Many examples of model legislation end up being passed into law in the states, word for word (www.brookings.edu/articles/alecs-influence-over-lawmaking-in-state -legislatures/), which is likely more indicative of imitation rather than of learning. Garrett and

the costs for states to learn about and adopt conservative laws on a variety of policy issues, an endeavor in which they have been quite successful. Whether promoting model laws or bringing policymakers together to discuss ideas, options, and successes – as supported by the National Conference of State Legislatures and the National Governors Association – facilitator organizations improve the chances for learning and diffusion.

Individuals also can be facilitators. Individual policy entrepreneurs identify problems, find innovative solutions, and build the coalitions necessary to bring their ideas to the attention of key policymakers. Such was the case in the 1990s when policy entrepreneurs began to advocate for school choice initiatives to address failing schools across the United States.[99] In response to this advocacy, states and school districts adopted vouchers for parents whose children opted out of public schools, created charter and magnet schools, and implemented several other reforms. Although not all of these reforms worked equally well, policy entrepreneurs helped bring about the experiments necessary for learning and also assisted in spreading the word about these policy options.

Overall, facilitators promote policy learning, whether as individuals like policy entrepreneurs, as organizations that are pushing for specific policies like the USGBC or ALEC, as media outlets facilitating the spread of information, or as governmental or nongovernmental organizations that bring different policymakers together. Conversely, the lack of facilitators can hinder the spread of a good policy. It should be kept in mind, however, that while policy entrepreneurs and interest groups can facilitate learning about the policies they favor, they also may impede diffusion of policies they oppose, even if such policies might be in the public interest.

3.6 When States Don't Learn, Other Diffusion Processes Take Over

In the previous subsections, we highlighted factors that might hinder learning and the spread of good policies. Now we consider three other mechanisms of diffusion that attain prominence when learning is either not available or not pursued. States might instead adopt policies because they are in *competition* with other states. States also might adopt policies because they are *imitating* what earlier states have done, perhaps to try to appear innovative themselves. Finally, diffusion also can occur due to *coercion*. In particular, the national government can force states to take actions or provide them with strong incentives to do so. Having already explained why the learning mechanism can (but might not) lead to the spread of good policies and limit the spread of bad

---

Jansa (2015) explore the importance of model legislation in policy diffusion, while Jansa, Hansen, and Gray (2019) examine the copy-and-paste approach to state lawmaking.

[99] See Mintrom (1997) and Mintrom and Vergari (1998).

policies, here we do the reverse and explain why diffusion based on these other mechanisms can make it easier for bad policies to spread while making it harder for good policies to do so.

3.6.1 Competition: Racing to the Bottom and Other Ailments

Competition can be beneficial. As we know from the private sector and capitalism in general, competition can encourage innovation, release creative energy, and generate new discoveries. Moving from the private to the public sphere, competition among states offers at least the potential of producing positive effects, which derive from adding market discipline to government policymaking.[100] If Virginia and Maryland are competing for businesses, they might develop new approaches to the use of tax incentives, approaches that bring companies to their states in a way that has a net positive effect on their overall financial health.[101] Or they might be moved to compete in the area of crime reduction, or to make housing easier to afford, or to create public goods like parks, all in an effort to promote new business startups in their state and to convince existing businesses to relocate there. Similarly, a city that learns that its residents are moving to surrounding communities so their children can attend better schools will have an incentive to improve its own school system or risk losing its tax base. Overall, competition can lead to more efficient processes and a reduction of waste or fraud.

However, competition also has a negative side. Consider the tendency of cities and states to subsidize sports franchises. The story is familiar: a team that has a long association with a city threatens to leave unless the city agrees to subsidize a replacement of the team's old, dilapidated stadium – or in many cases, their not-so-old, in-pretty-good-shape stadium, which just isn't quite as shiny or new as stadiums in other cities. Another city makes this threat credible by offering the team strong financial incentives to move. The team and its owner bluster about leaving, while the two cities – the team's current city and its potential new home – keep upping the ante to either attract or retain the team. Eventually, one city wins. Either the team stays, in which case the leaders in the losing city might be berated for not having done enough to attract the team, or it leaves, in which case fans in the current city talk about all of the financial devastation this will unleash upon their city – lost jobs, the spending during game weekends that is forgone, and so on.

---

[100] Tiebout (1956) presents the classic argument about competition and the sorting of individuals into different communities based on their preferences for public services and low taxes.

[101] Leiser (2017) explores the competitive pressures involved in the creation of business tax incentives.

Careful analyses, however, reveal that the benefits of new stadiums tend to be dramatically overstated, while the costs are understated.[102] Study after study reaches the same overall conclusion: "No recent facility appears to have earned anything approaching a reasonable return on investment."[103] Competition across governments leads to tax subsidies, but these subsidies lead to a net loss for the cities and their citizens.

The subsidization of sports teams provides a specific example of a more general phenomenon: competition can be destructive, exacerbating many of the problems discussed earlier. Competition motivates politicians to move quickly, without taking the requisite time to learn about which policies have worked best elsewhere and which will work best for them. They tend to pander to the public or cater to special interests. They tend to overstate positive effects of existing policies, while understating negative consequences. The availability and representative heuristics can be especially pernicious here, with states overgeneralizing from limited data about the effects of policies in other cities or inappropriately extrapolating from a small number of cases. More than anything, policymakers might be driven by the optics of the issue, worried more about passing policies that will look good rather than policies that actually will *be* good.

Competitive practices also can produce a "race to the bottom," a particularly problematic phenomenon for redistributive policies and social safety nets. For example, despite limited evidence of welfare recipients moving across state lines for additional payments, state policymakers fear that raising their benefit levels will make them "welfare magnets."[104] As such, they limit their welfare benefit levels to mimic those found in neighboring states and are hesitant to raise them in the face of inflation unless their neighbors act as well. Public health programs face similar pressures. While many Americans gain health insurance through their employers, others rely on Medicaid or the Affordable Care Act. Yet, politicians are often hesitant to raise taxes (which affect most voters) to support these programs (which benefit a smaller subset of voters), despite the broad public health benefits they offer.

Regulatory policies also are skewed by competitive pressures. Environmental and worker safety regulations that are costly to businesses may not be adopted,

---

[102] See Noll and Zimbalist (2011). Along these lines, sports economist Michael Leeds estimates that if every major sports team in Chicago – the Cubs, Bears, Bulls, Black Hawks, and White Sox – were to leave, the estimated financial hit to the city would be merely a fraction of 1 percent (www.kqed.org/news/10444227/new-nfl-team-unlikely-to-have-big-economic-impact-in-southern-california).

[103] www.brookings.edu/articles/sports-jobs-taxes-are-new-stadiums-worth-the-cost/

[104] For evidence of competition in health and welfare policies, see Peterson and Rom (1990), Volden (2002), and Bailey and Rom (2004).

due to fear of losing out to more attractive business environments in other states. Prison privatization policies spread across the states as a means of cutting expenses, leading to underfunding and poor conditions that harmed those who were viewed unfavorably by society.[105] Policies undergirding segregation and discrimination also proliferated through competitive pressures and policy diffusion.[106] From redlining policies – restricting loans and services provided to certain communities – to voting rights restrictions, numerous discriminatory policies spread quickly through US cities and states. This was especially true between the Civil War and the civil rights movement in the 1960s, and many of these policies have lingering effects today. When states are motivated by competition, rather than by learning, they will be more prone to adopt bad policies and less likely to adopt good ones.

3.6.2 Imitation: Flattery Will Get You Nowhere

States also might adopt policies because they are *imitating* (or mimicking) what earlier states have done. They may do so to give the impression of being innovative themselves. They might try to appear like another state, one that is highly regarded. Or perhaps they believe that adopting a policy will confer legitimacy upon them, that the policy is in some way normatively appealing and thus will show that the state is "doing the right thing." They jump on the bandwagon without necessarily recognizing the difference between what is popular and what is good.

What they do not do, in such circumstances, is *learn* about the policy. They do not observe multiple experiments, instead often just following the lead of one early-adopting state. They do not invest time and expertise, as they are not driven by learning whether a policy that has been successful is a good fit for their state. They merely observe that a policy was adopted elsewhere and then adopt it themselves.

This approach might lead to the adoption (and diffusion) of good policies. When this happens, it is by accident – a happy accident, but an accident nonetheless. If, for example, Florida has adopted a new set of health care policies for senior citizens and Arizona follows this initial action by adopting the same policy itself, it might be that Florida has chosen a good policy that ends up being appropriate for Arizona. However, it is also likely that such an approach will be problematic, that it can lead to the spread of ill-conceived, bad policies. At the same time, multiple good policies will be ignored in the process, remaining confined to the states that initially discovered them.

---

[105] See Hart, Shleifer, and Vishny (1997) for an assessment of prison privatization. Bouché and Volden (2011) explore the role of privatization in the spread of foster care policies.

[106] See Trounstine (2018) on the spread and perseverance of segregation and inequality.

Imitation can produce these negative consequences for a variety of reasons, two of which relate directly to the ingredients needed for successful learning (Figure 3). First, under imitation, states often move quickly to adopt new policies – too quickly to ascertain whether a policy is good. Sometimes they have no choice but to act with haste, as occurred with shutdown policies during the spring of 2020 in the face of COVID-19 outbreaks. Other times, imitation can occur because policies are highly salient, and state policymakers feel pressure – from citizens, groups, the media, political opponents – to do *something*, and to do it *now*. As we saw, three strikes laws fit this description to a T. State lawmakers quickly followed the initial movers and adopted this policy, with no evidence that it would reduce crime, with little consideration of its broader effects, and ignoring that crime was actually decreasing, not increasing, at the time.

Second, states might lack the expertise and incentives to learn. In some instances, this can work out in a satisfactory way. As we saw, even less-professional states were able to learn about how to reduce youth smoking rates and ended up adopting policies found in successful states.[107] Still, they did so with lower frequency than states with higher capacity and greater expertise. For policies that need to be tailored to particular circumstances – for example, policing should be responsive to the types of crime problems found in communities or job training should be tailored to employer needs – the one-size-fits-all policies brought through imitation are often problematic.

In sum, imitation fills in the gaps created when learning becomes too hard. When the effects of policies are tough to observe, when policymakers face near-term election pressures, when experts are unavailable, learning is difficult. As a result, policymakers muddle through, imitating readily available policies, many of which are ineffective or ill-suited to their own circumstances.

3.6.3 Coercion: If It Is Such a Good Idea, Why Do States Need to Be Coerced into Action?

Finally, policies also spread due to *coercion*. For example, the national government can force states to take actions with regulations and unfunded mandates or provide them with strong incentives to do so with intergovernmental grants.[108] To be clear, the federal government can take actions that increase the ability of states to learn. As we discussed earlier, Congress can shine a bright spotlight on policy

---

[107] Shipan and Volden (2008) find a similar pattern across cities, with smaller communities copying whatever smoking restrictions their larger neighboring cities adopted, whereas larger cities demonstrated the capability to explore options and learn from others.

[108] See Posner (1998) on federal government unfunded mandates and Oates (1999) on intergovernmental grant incentives.

issues and options, which can increase opportunities to learn. Conversely, the absence of federal action can create a space in which states are forced to seek out information about policy options, such as we saw with the failure of the national government to develop a coherent approach to dealing with the pandemic in 2020.

In large part, however, the role of the federal government in diffusion operates through coercion. Such coercive pressures can cause states to grudgingly adopt policies that might not be well suited for their needs. That said, as with the other non-learning mechanisms of diffusion, there can be circumstances where such coercion plays a positive role in promoting learning or countering negative competition. For example, the Synar Amendment coerced states to tackle youth smoking, setting off a wave of experimentation and learning. As another example, given the underinvestment in social safety net programs across the states due to competitive pressures and tight budgets, federal Medicaid grants match state spending at higher rates in poorer states like Mississippi. This process allows such states the opportunity to expand their programs to levels they would desire in the absence of competition or if they had greater financial resources.

More typically, however, grants and other coercive measures distort policies away from what state policymakers would prefer to do, instead leading them to adopt policies that are inappropriate for their own circumstances. National highway grants were used to coerce states to adopt fifty-five-mile-per-hour speed limits, even in parts of North Dakota so empty and so flat that drivers can see the curvature of the earth on the horizon.[109] They also induced states to adopt drinking ages that many policymakers (and teenagers) viewed as striking the wrong balance between individual freedom and public safety.

A recent example of national-to-state coercion occurred in the implementation of the Affordable Care Act (ACA). To induce states to expand their Medicaid programs to families above the federal poverty level, the ACA provided national funding for more than 90 percent of the cost of the expansion. Many state policymakers in conservative states argued that the expansion was not appropriate for their states. Instead of encouraging market pressures to hold down health care costs, Medicaid was seen as entrenching a cost structure that was divorced from the reality of how much doctor visits, medical procedures, and hospitalization actually cost. Although they initially held out against expanding their programs, more and more states eventually found it politically costly to forgo the federal outlays over time and began adopting Medicaid expansions.[110] Of course, a strong case can be made for the benefits of such

---

[109] One of the authors of this book enjoyed such vistas for eighteen years, before sampling what it was like to live in other states.

[110] On the coverage effects of ACA policies, see Frean, Gruber, and Sommers (2017).

an expansion. But to the extent that states should be allowed to adopt whatever health insurance policies they feel best reflect their local needs and circumstances, federal coercion was instead forcing more uniform standards.

Coercion also arises within states, such as when states preempt any separate policy choices across localities. For instance, fearful of local authorities adopting what they perceived as the "wrong" policies in response to COVID-19, most governors shut all schools in their states, and some governors reversed local government policies requiring residents to wear masks in public places. In Virginia, state laws restricted the ability of local governments to remove Confederate statues from their parks and plazas despite the history of racism behind the erection of many such statues. When many localities were the first movers in adopting anti-smoking policies, a number of state governments acted quickly (pressured by tobacco interests) to place limits on local authorities to act.

In each case, states and localities were prevented (or highly discouraged) from learning about other policy options, evaluating how effective they might be, and embracing successes while abandoning failures. Other governments, believing they knew better, instead short-circuited such a process of discovery and coerced these states and localities toward specific actions that they likely would not have taken on their own.

3.7 A Long List of Learning Limitations

The case for the learning-based spread of good policies is straightforward and compelling. States have the opportunity to experiment with policies. Some experiments work; some do not. As other states look across the country, they are drawn to the successes and avoid the failures. As a result, good policies spread, while bad ones do not. As shown in Figure 3, this recipe for success relies on three main ingredients – observable experiments, time to learn, and proper incentives and expertise. But, as this section suggests, this recipe can go wrong in many, many ways.

Table 2 lists the reasons why this recipe may go astray, each of which – eighteen in all – we have discussed in some detail. The table also links each reason to the key ingredients for learning-based success. For example, observable experiments are undermined when policymakers instead rely on the availability and representativeness heuristics or when facilitators do not spread the word about experiments elsewhere. Time to learn is hampered by legislators spending little time in session or being pressured into short-term thinking. Expertise is limited when legislators lack staff support, especially when facing complex policy areas. In all, this list makes a compelling case that, under many

Table 2 Problems for the learning-based spread of good policies

What Could Go Wrong?	*Problem Area*
Policy Attributes	
1. Policies are not observable	Observable Experiments
2. Policies lack clear relative advantages	Time to Learn
3. Policy is too complex	Expertise/Incentives
4. Policy is incompatible with current practices	Expertise/Incentives
5. Policy is low salience	Time to Learn
6. Policy lacks trialability	Expertise/Incentives
Biased Policymaking	
7. Policymakers face short-term thinking	Time to Learn
8. Policymakers pander to voters	Expertise/Incentives
9. Policymakers cater to contributors and special interests	Expertise/Incentives
10. Policymakers rely too much on availability	Observable Experiments
11. Policymakers view limited examples as representative	Observable Experiments
Political Processes	
12. Legislators lack expert staff and committees	Expertise/Incentives
13. Legislators spend too little time in session	Time to Learn
14. Salary insufficient to attract effective policymakers	Expertise/Incentives
15. Policy lacks facilitators of learning and change	Observable Experiments
Mechanisms Beyond Learning	
16. Competition replaces learning	Expertise/Incentives
17. Policymakers rely on imitation	Time to Learn
18. Policymakers face coercion	Expertise/Incentives

different circumstances, good policies will not spread, while bad policy choices may flourish.

Returning to our opening example of criminal sentencing guidelines, we find many reasons why things went wrong. To name but a few, determinate sentencing often lacked clear relative advantages over the prior system, the effects of which would not be observed until many years down the road. Instead, policymakers relied on short-term thinking, often pandering to voters with tough-on-crime policies just prior to elections. Once some states adopted three strikes and similar policies, others did not want to look out of step or weak. Such policies were readily available and perceived as representative. States then imitated one another without taking time to learn whether these policies were succeeding or failing.

Such a long list of what could go wrong may seem daunting, likely to doom all prospects for learning and for the spread of good policies. At a systemic level, this list draws into question not just the ability of any single state to learn from others but also the entire enterprise of the states in American federalism serving as effective policy laboratories at all. We do not hold such a pessimistic view ourselves, however. Rather than viewing this list as making the case that policymaking in US federalism is hopeless, we see this list as providing clarity about how the system could be improved. In the next section, we offer a series of lessons for those looking to spread good policies and potential reforms that may help us get closer to that ideal setting in which good policies spread and bad ones don't.

4 Back to the Laboratory

4.1 What Have We Learned about Learning?

Because our argument involves many pieces – federalism, biases in policy-making, politicians and their incentives, political institutions, states, facilitators, and more – it might seem complicated. But in reality, it is straightforward. The normatively appealing promise of policymaking in a federal system is that good policies will spread, while bad ones won't. This outcome can occur because some states will conduct policy experiments "without risk to the rest of the country," as Brandeis put it. Other states will then learn which of these experimental policies were successful and will adopt the good ones and avoid the bad.

Does policymaking under US federalism actually unfold in this way? We argue that it *can*. But that is much different from arguing that it *will*. To this point, we contend that three main ingredients allow for the learning-based spread of good policies – and hinder the spread of bad policies. First, observable policy experiments need to take place. If no states are willing to experiment, then others will have no opportunity to learn. Nor will states have the opportunity to learn if these early experiments and their effects fly under the radar.

Second, states need time to be able to learn from earlier observed experiments. In some circumstances, policymakers in other states will not have time to learn about which policies are good and which are not. States might experience pressure to act immediately, as we saw with stay-at-home orders during the initial stages of the COVID-19 outbreak, or internal political pressures might push politicians to act quickly on highly salient policies, as we saw with three strikes policies. When state policymakers want or need to act quickly, they lose the ability to determine which policies worked well elsewhere and, more specifically, which policies will work well for them.

Third, states need expertise and the right incentives to learn from earlier experiments. That is, state institutions must help policymakers develop the expertise necessary for evaluating policies, and state policymakers must have the proper incentives to do so. State legislatures that have well-designed standing committees, hire more staffers, pay well, and meet regularly create an environment in which lawmakers can develop and apply expertise to the assessment of policies. Meanwhile, legislators who are able to avoid biases common in politics – biases described by the availability and representativeness heuristics, tendencies to pander to voters or cater to special interests, and short-term rather than long-term thinking – are better able to engage in learning.

Even with these three ingredients in hand – observable experiments, time to learn, and expertise combined with proper incentives – learning still is not guaranteed. Beyond biased policymaking and political institutions that limit expertise, sometimes the characteristics of policies themselves (like their complexity or incompatibility) and the tendency to rely on imitation or competition can get in the way of learning. For learning to occur, and for good policies to spread, a surprising number of pieces need to be in place. In the absence of one of these pieces, learning might not occur, causing good policies to languish, with success in the initial states that passed them but then not moving beyond those states.

Learning, therefore, is possible yet difficult. It can occur, but it might not. Throughout this concluding section, we reflect on the lessons that emerge from the previous sections and highlight nine concrete steps that policy actors – whether at the national level or in the states, whether policymakers or facilitators – can take to help realize the promise of US federalism. We then end where we began – with the COVID-19 pandemic – and an assessment of whether, when, and where these lessons have been learned during one of the most trying times for state policymaking.

4.2 Lessons for All Actors across American Federalism

As Table 2 makes clear, many things can go wrong despite best efforts to ensure the spread of good public policies across the states. In this section, we outline how policymakers might address these problems. We lead off our prescriptions with two lessons for all actors in the federal system.

Lesson #1: *All actors in the federal system can work to improve the observability of policy experiments.*

Observability, as we have discussed, is necessary for the learning-based diffusion of good policies. When a policy is not observed, no learning can take place. When it is observed, learning is a possibility (although not a certainty). What can be done to help states observe the policy successes of others and to avoid their failures? Three clear opportunities emerge. First, the national government can increase the observability of state policies, as it did with the Synar Amendment's requirement that states report outcome measures regarding youth smoking. Common reporting mandates, coupled with the financial support to follow those mandates, provide clarity regarding which states are succeeding on key measures, while countering the availability heuristic by highlighting options beyond those immediately at hand. Second, the states themselves can make their actions and policy successes more observable through media attention or by working with other actors like the National Governors Association. Third, facilitators can increase observability. Few states or local governments understood their options for green buildings or the success of these options before the USGBC stepped in with clear, observable standards.

Lesson #2: *All actors in the federal system can point out the relative advantages of new policy options.*

Much of learning involves exploring which policy variant in a specific area offers the greatest relative advantage over current policy. This takes time. Once again, facilitators and policy experts at all levels of government can help. Often that help involves problem definition.[111] Is the greatest concern in developing a health care policy finding ways to increase coverage, to lower costs, or to increase quality of care? By clarifying where the greatest room for improvement in a state (or across all states) exists, policy experts also shape the evaluative criteria for determining whether a policy change is good or bad – and whether it will achieve its greatest relative advantage. Taking the time up front to define program goals can help focus the learning process on the most important elements, saving time later on and promoting learning.

4.3 Lessons for National Policymakers

Although the preceding recommendations offer a call to action across the federal system, some actions undergirding states as policy laboratories specifically require national government attention.

Lesson #3: *National policymakers can heighten the salience of policy challenges.*

As we explained in Section 3.3, the effect of salience is complicated. For low-salience issues, policymakers might feel little pressure to act and thus

---

[111] Gilardi, Shipan, and Wüest (2021) show how diffusion influences the ways in which policy issues are defined.

a negligible incentive to learn about policy experiments conducted elsewhere. Ironically, high levels of salience also can hinder learning by pressing policy-makers to act before any learning has taken place, as we saw with three strikes laws. National politicians are uniquely positioned to raise the salience of pressing policy problems that have not yet achieved urgency in the states. Presidents can discuss them in State of the Union addresses. Congressional committees can hold hearings. The Supreme Court can issue rulings defining the latitude that states have to refine their policies. Each action affects whether citizens and state policymakers take notice of a problem. For example, when President George W. Bush gave a nationally televised address in 2001 on the issue of stem cell research, the number of stem cell bills in state legislatures rose substantially.[112] When Congress held hearings on tobacco issues, states became more active in addressing this issue.[113]

Lesson #4: *National policymakers can structure intergovernmental grants to counteract competition while avoiding coercion.*

We highlighted how in the presence of competition states might cut their spending in redistributive areas, such as health care and welfare, relative to what they would offer were there no "race to the bottom" pressures. The federal government can act to offset some of these competitive pressures across states. Most prominently, enforcement of the US Constitution's Commerce Clause keeps states from erecting trade barriers and otherwise limiting economic activities across states.[114] Additionally, in specific policy areas, federal grants can counter incentives produced by competition. Federal cost-sharing through matching grants can realign state incentives for redistributive programs to levels they would normally pursue absent state-to-state competition.[115] As with any grant program, however, care must be taken to limit the coercion put forward in grant requirements. Coercion that promotes policy experimentation and learning across states, as with youth smoking innovations, may be beneficial. However, when national policymakers overuse their financial powers to influence state actions toward unproven uniform standards, governors need to push back forcefully.[116]

---

[112] See Karch's (2012) insightful examination of stem-cell policymaking.

[113] Clouser McCann, Shipan, and Volden (2015) show that national government discussions about smoking policies increased state anti-smoking adoptions.

[114] Wiseman and Ellig (2007) evaluate the economic benefits of the Commerce Clause by examining the trade barriers surrounding the wine industry.

[115] Wilde (1971) describes the shift in incentives through different types of grant programs.

[116] Cammisa (1995) discusses how state governments can act as interest groups to affect national policy decisions.

Lesson #5: *National policymakers can promote a diversity of experimental models across states.*

When state governments do not vocally object to national mandates, their room for experimentation may be cut significantly. Imposing the same speed limits in all states provides one such example. In contrast, welfare reforms in the mid-1990s set off a wave of state experimentation, as did funding for children's health insurance programs. Some fear that programs like the Affordable Care Act in 2010, however, cut short a wave of state experimentation by including too many specific details regarding state health care offerings. This is not to say that the national government should stay on the sidelines when states are unwilling to act or when state policies are discriminatory. The Civil Rights Act and Voting Rights Act in the 1960s, for example, were crucial in ending discriminatory policies. Rather, we point out that nationwide standards in areas where states are legitimately searching for the best policy solutions could undermine such experimentation.

4.4 Lessons for State Policymakers

Beyond national government actions, states themselves have a major role to play in setting their own course as effective policy laboratories. Indeed, as the leading actors in this drama, they must constantly hone their skills to perform well.

Lesson #6: *States can adopt institutional reforms to limit biases and cultivate expertise.*

Table 2 listed many of the biases that state policymakers confront, as well as the limitations that many states face in developing sufficient policy expertise. Cultivating expertise and the right incentives often means protecting or even reforming state institutions. Staggered legislative terms for senators and different term lengths across elected politicians' offices limit the extent to which all politicians share the same short-term, election-driven pressures at the same time. Term limits on legislators may make the problem worse, giving lawmakers an added sense of urgency that yields imitation rather than learning.

The creation of policy-specific standing committees, the hiring and cultivation of experienced legislative staff, and longer legislative sessions all promote the development of expertise. Higher salaries attract more qualified candidates for office. Not everyone wants legislatures to feature these characteristics, however, which is why many states lack one or more of them. These states appeal to the notion of a citizen legislature, which some people find attractive. The features of a citizen legislature make it less likely that politicians will have long legislative careers, giving more people an opportunity to serve in government, possibly bringing in new ideas and tying legislative behavior more closely to average citizens. However, citizen legislatures come at a cost: they typically lack the expertise found in more professional legislatures and, therefore, are less able to learn about successful policies enacted elsewhere.

Lesson #7: *State policymakers can seek the help of policy experts in a wide array of settings.*

When state policymakers lack expertise in specific areas, they need to be unafraid to ask for help. New problems always arise, and no legislator can keep on top of all of the constantly evolving issues. As such, legislators need to develop ways to fill in gaps in their knowledge. One possibility involves building up norms around the use of experts and commissions. If a state adopts a standard practice of in-depth study through hearings and markups in legislative committees or of setting up independent commissions to advance policy proposals for major issues, then attempts to short-circuit such processes to engage in imitation or to advance an ill-advised politically motivated agenda will be treated with skepticism. Policy entrepreneurs and facilitators can play a central role here. Faced with time pressures and a need to act, those who already possess substantial expertise can help policymakers find a timely solution without sacrificing learning.[117]

The reforms needed to increase state policymaking expertise are therefore fairly straightforward – either take steps to professionalize the legislature or find sources of expertise apart from the legislature itself. However, relying on policy entrepreneurs and special interests may reintroduce the biases in their favor that we discussed earlier. Relying on experts in bureaucratic agencies may cede policy control to the executive branch. Where neutral policy specialists exist outside of government, their valuable expertise can be gained through their involvement in legislative hearings or independent commissions.

4.5 Lessons for Policymaking Facilitators

As just mentioned, policymaking facilitators can help states function more effectively as policy laboratories. To do so, they must take care to provide the most valuable information in the right way at the right time.

Lesson #8: *Facilitators can explain complex policies and link problems to solutions.*

As we have noted, complex problems that need to be addressed with insufficient time for study present a nightmare scenario for state policymakers. Fortunately, facilitators like interest groups and policy entrepreneurs possess just the sorts of skills and knowledge needed in such circumstances. Because

---

[117] Mintrom (1997, 2019) shows the benefit of relying on education policy entrepreneurs to spread policies from state to state. Anderson, DeLeo, and Taylor (2020) explore the role of entrepreneurs in agenda setting.

they often have focused on a single issue for a long time, facilitators have the specialized knowledge needed to convey complex information in a clear-cut way. Moreover, because they have been seeking – and advocating for – specific policy solutions, they are highly motivated to find ways to link those solutions to particular problems in new and compelling ways.[118] They are also typically up-to-date in knowing which policies have been tried elsewhere and whether they have been successful. Consequently, the expertise of facilitators can substitute for a lack of internal expertise, providing information about policies and outcomes elsewhere.[119] Especially for policies with low trialability – those that are difficult to attempt and cannot be easily abandoned once underway – facilitators can offer crucial help in avoiding pitfalls.

Lesson #9: *Facilitators can help draw conclusions from preliminary data, showing which solutions are generalizable and which must be tailored to specific conditions.*

Finally, facilitators also offer assistance that may speed up learning opportunities. Being able to assess policies in a timely manner and to draw conclusions while evidence is still coming in may help set policymakers on the right course.[120] Of course, state policymakers should maintain a degree of skepticism in accepting their aid. In-depth conversations should involve discussions of why the emerging evidence suggests that a specific reform is promising, as well as why those results likely indicate that the policy will work just as well here as it did elsewhere. What might be different about another state's infrastructure policy experiences, for example, and how should the policy be adjusted to local circumstances and conditions? Facilitators enable the spread of information, but policymakers set policies and must therefore accept the help of experts in a discerning manner.

On the whole, we have established the three main ingredients needed in the recipe for policymaking success. We have highlighted eighteen ways this recipe could go awry across four categories of concern. And we have suggested nine lessons that policymakers can take away to help mitigate these problems. Ultimately, however, the proof of the pudding comes in the tasting. How well does the US federal system live up to its promise in these most challenging of times?

---

[118] This is similar to Kingdon's (1995) well-known idea that solutions can exist independent of problems, with policy entrepreneurs (and other political actors) waiting for the right moment to promote those solutions.

[119] Of course, this comes with some risk, as facilitators may push for policies from a very specific point of view. A liberal think tank, for example, might provide information about the benefits of green energy programs without also acknowledging problems that have emerged in states that have adopted such policies.

[120] Bromley-Trujillo and Karch (2019) show that scientific uncertainty slows the spread of policies.

4.6 The Laboratories of Democracy Meet a Global Pandemic

We conclude our study of the spread of good or bad policies back where we began. Throughout 2020 and 2021, state policymakers dealt with the COVID-19 pandemic, with bleak initial prospects for the learning-based spread of good public policies. Since all states were confronting the novel coronavirus at the same time, there were no previous observable state experiments to learn from at the onset of this public health crisis, and there was little expert knowledge in terms of how the novel virus spread, how deadly it was, or how to stop it.

As policymakers began to work through the problems, however, glimmers of hope began to emerge. Governors bought time through the drastic measures of shutting schools and government offices, then issuing stay-at-home orders soon thereafter. Many (although not all) state governments then called on infectious disease experts within their states or nationwide to develop a plan of action. Facilitators arose to serve as clearinghouses for best practices, documenting what was tried in other states and how those practices affected their infection rates, treatments, and outcomes. With such conditions in hand, learning and the spread of good policies *could* occur. But did it? Keeping in mind our daunting list of all that could still go wrong, with little room for error, did states learn the right lessons and adopt good policies found elsewhere?

We answer these questions by examining one policy option considered across the states during the coronavirus pandemic. Specifically, we focus on the decision to require residents to wear masks in public and in businesses throughout the state. We assess how well state policymakers (mainly governors) confronted the many obstacles to learning-based policy diffusion. Did they learn the right lessons and overcome these challenges? And how did the national government and policy facilitators help or hinder their efforts? Of course, this constitutes but a single policy example, so an examination of mask mandate decisions does not provide a definitive test of the argument we advance. But mask mandates do exemplify the potential promise and peril of policymaking within US federalism.

State policymakers had a number of policy options available to them throughout the initial months of the pandemic. These ranged from closing schools, public buildings, or all nonessential businesses, to adopting vigorous tracking and tracing programs, to various quarantining practices, to mandating social distancing and mask wearing. Each came with a set of costs and benefits, in terms of direct financial costs, of limiting the spread of the virus, and of harming the economy.[121] How "good" each policy was on these dimensions was initially uncertain. Over the

---

[121] Again, although these were usually the primary considerations, they were not the only ones. Protecting liberty, addressing equity issues, and enhancing education also were prominent.

summer of 2020, strong evidence emerged that many of these practices worked well in combination but also that perhaps the single most cost-effective means for preventing disease transmission was the widespread wearing of masks.[122] This evidence emerged from laboratory studies as well as from observational evidence about which states and countries adopted each policy prescription and when. Although far from a singular silver bullet, mask mandates plainly had positive effects and were part of the solution. When you add in their low cost relative to other policy options, mask mandates easily meet our definition of good policy.[123]

How well did public policy actors follow the lessons highlighted here to help the states learn about this policy's effectiveness and to contribute to its spread from one state to the next? The first two lessons we offered suggest that all actors in the federal system can work to increase the observability of policy experiments and to highlight their relative advantages. Facilitators in this area were numerous, ranging from associations of state governments to media outlets.[124] Hence, it was easy to observe which states were acting and when. Governors themselves heightened the observability of their policy choices with widely publicized and regularly held press conferences. With regard to masks specifically, studies of the relative effectiveness of mask mandates were conducted and published in prominent outlets like the *Journal of the American Medical Association* and *Health Affairs*, then covered broadly in the media. The lone failure in emphasizing the relative advantage of mask mandates came from the national government, such as with the Centers for Disease Control and Prevention (CDC) initially opposing mask wearing for months and only endorsing this policy in mid-July.[125] This change in position seemed to matter. Over the four months prior to the CDC recommendation, twenty-three states had slowly adopted mask mandates. In the two weeks following the CDC switch, ten more quickly followed suit.

These lessons also suggest a prominent role for the national government in raising the salience of policy problems and potential solutions, in offering well-designed intergovernmental grants, and in promoting diverse experiments across the states. With respect to salience, little needed to be done, as COVID-19 quickly became the top policy priority within the states and around

---

[122] Evidence pointing to these conclusions was summarized in www.ucsf.edu/news/2020/06/417906/still-confused-about-masks-heres-science-behind-how-face-masks-prevent and www.healthaffairs.org/doi/10.1377/hlthaff.2020.00818.

[123] Some may argue that this judgment downplays the role of individual liberty. Current politicized views of individual liberty as "doing as we like," however, stand in direct contrast to the well-founded and long-standing ethical tradition defining individual liberty as "doing as we like as long as it *does not* harm others" (see Mill 1859).

[124] Both the National Conference of State Legislatures and the National Governors Association compiled thorough records of state pandemic policies, as did several news outlets.

[125] See www.cnn.com/2020/07/14/health/coronavirus-masks-cdc-editorial/index.html.

the world, despite President Trump's frequent attempts to downplay the pandemic.[126] Federal funding to states also came quickly, with more than $300 billion of the $2 trillion CARES Act passed in March 2020 directed to support state and local governments. Although this effort did not directly address mask mandates, it did give states leeway to experiment with a variety of different policies.

Perhaps the main limit on state experiments came from the heightened political polarization arising during a presidential election year.[127] President Trump, for example, refused to wear a mask in public through the initial months of the pandemic.[128] Many Republican voters followed the president's lead in downplaying the seriousness of the pandemic and advocating for fewer restrictions on businesses and individuals, including opposition to mask mandates. As a result, prior to the CDC changing its recommendations and to the president wearing a mask in public for the first time on July 11, only four states with Republican governors issued mask mandates, compared with nineteen states with Democratic governors doing the same.[129]

At the state level, our lessons involve, first, making institutional reforms to limit biases and enhance expertise and, second, seeking help from experts. Given the speed of the pandemic, major institutional reforms were out of the question. But some states took steps to counter the partisan bias behind the adoption of mask mandates.[130] Gov. Larry Hogan (R-MD), for example, was an early adopter and strong advocate, saying, "Wearing masks is the single best mitigation strategy that we have to fight the virus, and the science and data are very clear."[131] Gov. Greg Abbott (R-TX) issued a mask mandate as a desperation move to keep from having to lock the state down entirely in the face of a major surge in cases across Texas over the summer. On the whole, however, these steps were insufficient to overcome the broader partisan policy

---

[126] Woodward's (2020) interviews with the president reveal that Trump's strategy was to downplay the pandemic to keep the American people from panicking.

[127] In contrast, Germany's response appeared to be more forceful and coherent in 2020, only foundering as it entered its high-stakes election year in 2021 (see www.nytimes.com/2021/02/11/opinion/germany-covid-second-wave.html).

[128] For coverage of President Trump's mask-wearing behavior, see www.politico.com/news/2020/07/11/trum-wears-face-mask-walter-reed-visit-357249.

[129] Adolph et al. (2021) show that states led by Republican governors also were slower to implement social distancing policies. Doing so may have been politically risky. On the whole, governors who adopted mask mandates and other strong mitigation practices seemed to receive major boosts in public opinion ratings, compared with those who were less aggressive on this front: www.washingtonpost.com/politics/2020/07/31/governors-took-strict-measures-coronavirus-are-seeing-better-political-outcomes/.

[130] See Linder et al. (2020) for evidence regarding the partisan spread of policies across numerous policy areas.

[131] www.washingtonpost.com/local/dc-adjusts-key-metric-as-officials-monitor-future-move-to-next-recovery-phase/2020/07/29/2f18fe04-d1a2-11ea-8d32-1ebf4e9d8e0d_story.html

bias. By August 1, 2020, all twenty-four Democratic governors had issued mask mandates, while only about one-third of Republican governors (nine of twenty-six) had done so. Throughout the fall and winter pandemic surges, another half dozen Republican-led states adopted mask mandates, while others quickly abandoned them early in 2021.[132]

Many (although not all) states performed much better with respect to bringing in experts. Internally, they relied on public health and infectious diseases experts, with many setting up advisory groups. They sought advice from facilitators outside their states, from the national government and the private sector. Our lessons suggest that such facilitators promote the spread of good public policies when they help explain complex policies, link problems to solutions, and draw well-grounded conclusions from preliminary data. On these fronts, mask mandates are not terribly complex. Yet facilitators played critical roles in explaining why broad mask wearing was crucial not just among those showing active symptoms but also among all persons (due to the contagiousness of asymptomatic people). They discussed the different types of masks and their various benefits. And they were able to show that preliminary results of lab experiments and mask-wearing experiments in a small number of states and countries all pointed in the direction of this policy's effectiveness.

On the whole, the United States had some clear failures and clear successes in its pandemic response. The country was ill-prepared and under-equipped from the start. Stay-at-home orders were not issued in time to avoid outbreaks that eventually occurred in every state; then the orders that were issued led to a major economic downturn. In some areas, nursing homes were not given extra attention and protection; rather, in states like New York, ill patients were sent to these facilities to recover, seeding further outbreaks and deaths. On the positive side of the ledger, economic hardship was reduced by massive federal aid packages (which of course will need to be paid for one day), and the Trump administration's Operation Warp Speed for vaccine development was a remarkable and unprecedented success. At the state level, a combination of responses worked well in some places, offering lessons for others.

In terms of mask mandates, we would argue that US federalism performed well, although not perfectly. In the early months, conditions were ripe for policy failure – no observable experiments, no time to learn, limited expertise, and biased incentives. But seven states experimented with mask mandates in April 2020, joined by another seven states in May. Data from these states' experiments became available in June, influencing expert opinion by July.

---

[132] Partisanship also played a significant role in vaccination rates across individuals and states in 2021, with Democrats much more likely than Republicans to be vaccinated.

Facilitators and experts then made a substantial push for state action. By early August, in a country that had not embraced widespread mask wearing in more than a century, two-thirds of the states had mask mandates in place.[133] A more complete spread of this policy would likely have come if the issue had not been swept up in election year hyper-partisanship. But many of the states without such a policy by the fall of 2020 had experienced low initial infection rates, making them less prone to adopt such a policy, and many featured cultures that placed a heavy weight on individual freedom. Moreover, by another standard, the federal system likely outperformed a centralized system in which mask mandate policies were solely set at the national level, since President Trump's anti-mask position coupled with divided government likely would have led to no mask mandates at all.

4.7 Final Thoughts

Whether approaching slow-spreading issues like anti-smoking restrictions or crisis management in a pandemic, we argue that the system of American federalism promises that good policies will spread across the states and bad ones will be dismissed. Such a happy outcome arises from learning-based policy diffusion. Central to such good outcomes are the three ingredients of observable experiments, time to learn, and the proper incentives and expertise of policymakers.

While these three ingredients are often plentiful in US federalism, we highlighted four areas in which the recipe for success can – and often does – go awry. First, the attributes of policies – from their complexity to their incompatibility with current practices – can undermine their spread. Second, numerous biases in policymaking mitigate against learning. Third, political and institutional considerations – including shortages of expertise, policymaking capacity, and facilitators – limit the ability to learn from others. Finally, when learning is absent, competition, imitation, and coercion can allow bad policies to spread while good ones do not. Collectively, these four causes for concern explain why attempts at learning from others can go wrong.

Countering these concerns are lessons to be learned by reformers and policymakers at every level of government. The extent to which US federalism can fulfill its promise, with states serving as policy laboratories, depends on whether such laboratories continue to work as they should. Absent efforts to cultivate and encourage experimentation, to provide time to learn from successes, and to endow policymakers with proper incentives and expertise, bad policies will spread while good ones won't.

---

[133] For details of mask wearing during the 1918 flu pandemic and its lessons for 2020, see www.healthaffairs.org/do/10.1377/hblog20200508.769108/full/.

In our view, the lessons and reforms that we highlight here will follow the same path as all of the good policies discussed throughout this study. Some states will adopt reforms to increase their policymaking expertise and reduce their biases, while others will continue their current practices. Those who adopt our suggested reforms will be better able to confront policy problems and to learn from others in the future. We hope that their successes will be sufficient to encourage others to likewise clean up their laboratories and get back to work.

References

Adolph, Christopher, Kenya Amano, Bree Bang-Jensen, Nancy Fullman, and John Wilkerson. 2021. Pandemic politics: Timing state-level social distancing responses to COVID-19. *Journal of Health Politics, Policy and Law* 46 (2): 211–233.

Alciati, Marianne H., Marcy Frosh, Sylvan B. Green, Ross C. Brownson, Peter H. Fisher, Robin Hobart, Adele Roman, Russell C. Sciandra, and Dana M. Shelton. 1998. State laws on youth access to tobacco in the United States: Measuring their extensiveness with a new rating system. *Tobacco Control* 7: 345–352.

Anderson, Sarah E., Rob A. DeLeo, and Kristin Taylor. 2020. Policy entrepreneurs, legislators, and agenda setting: Information and influence. *Policy Studies Journal* 48(3): 587–611.

Bailey, Michael A., and Mark C. Rom. 2004. A wider race? Interstate competition across health and welfare programs. *Journal of Politics* 66 (2): 326–347.

Bednar, Jenna. 2015. The Resilience of the American Federal System. In Mark Tushnet, Mark A. Graber, and Sanford Levinson, eds., pp. 283–302, *The Oxford Handbook of the US Constitution*. New York: Oxford University Press.

Berry, Frances Stokes, and William D. Berry. 1990. State lottery adoptions as policy innovations: An event history analysis. *American Political Science Review* 84(2): 395–415.

Berry, Frances Stokes, and William D. Berry. 1992. Tax innovation in the states: Capitalizing on political opportunity. *American Journal of Political Science* 36(3): 715–742.

Billard, Côme, Anna Creti, and Antoine Mandel. 2020. How environmental policies spread: A network approach to diffusion in the U.S. *FAERE Working Paper*, 2020.12.

Boehmke, Frederick J., and Paul Skinner. 2012. State policy innovativeness revisited. *State Politics and Policy Quarterly* 12(3): 303–329.

Bouché, Vanessa, and Craig Volden. 2011. Privatization and the diffusion of innovations. *Journal of Politics* 73(2): 428–442.

Boushey, Graeme. 2010. *Policy Diffusion Dynamics in America*. Cambridge: Cambridge University Press.

Bramson, Heidi, Don C. Des Jarlais, Kamyar Arasteh, Ann Nugent, Vivian Guardino, Jonathan Feelemyer, and Derek Hodel. 2015. State laws, syringe exchange, and HIV among persons who inject drugs in the United States: History and effectiveness. *Journal of Public Health Policy* 36(2): 212–230.

Brandeis, Louis Dembitz. 1932. Dissenting opinion. *New State Ice Co. v. Liebmann*, 285 US 262, 311.

Bricker, Christine, and Scott LaCombe. 2021. The ties that bind us: The influence of perceived state similarity on policy diffusion. *Political Research Quarterly* 74(2): 377–387.

Bromley-Trujillo, Rebecca, and Andrew Karch. 2019. Salience, scientific uncertainty, and the agenda-setting power of science. *Policy Studies Journal*. https://onlinelibrary.wiley.com/doi/full/10.1111/psj.12373.

Bucchianeri, Peter, Craig Volden, and Alan E. Wiseman. 2020. *Legislative effectiveness in the American states*. Working paper: Center for Effective Lawmaking, https://thelawmakers.org

Butler, Daniel M., Craig Volden, Adam M. Dynes, and Boris Shor. 2017. Ideology, learning, and policy diffusion: Experimental evidence. *American Journal of Political Science* 61(1): 37–49.

Callander, Steven. 2011. Searching for good policies. *American Political Science Review* 105(4): 643–662.

Cammisa, Anne Marie. 1995. *Governments as Interest Groups: Intergovernmental Lobbying and the Federal System*. Westport, CT: Praeger.

Clouser McCann, Pamela J., and Charles R. Shipan. How many major laws delegate to federal agencies? (Almost) all of them. *Political Science Research and Methods*. Forthcoming.

Clouser McCann, Pamela J., Charles R. Shipan, and Craig Volden. 2015. Top-down federalism: State policy responses to national government discussions. *Publius: The Journal of Federalism* 45(4): 495–525.

Enns, Peter K. 2014. The public's increasing punitiveness and its influence on mass incarceration in the United States. *American Journal of Political Science* 58(4): 857–872.

Eshbaugh-Soha, Matthew. 2006. The conditioning effects of policy salience and complexity on American political institutions. *Policy Studies Journal* 34(2): 223–243.

Fay, Daniel L., and Jeffrey B. Wenger. 2016. The political structure of policy diffusion. *Policy Studies Journal* 44(3): 349–365.

Frean, Molly, Jonathan Gruber, and Benjamin D. Sommers. 2017. Premium subsidies, the mandate, and Medicaid expansion: Coverage effects of the Affordable Care Act. *Journal of Health Economics* 53: 72–86.

Füglister, Katharina. 2012. Where does learning take place? The role of inter-governmental cooperation in policy diffusion. *European Journal of Political Research* 51(3): 316–349.

Garrett, Kristin N., and Joshua M. Jansa. 2015. Interest group influence in policy diffusion networks. *State Politics and Policy Quarterly* 15(3): 387–417.

Gilardi, Fabrizio, Charles R. Shipan, and Bruno Wüest. 2021. Policy diffusion: The issue definition stage. *American Journal of Political Science* 65(1): 21–35.

Gilens, Martin, and Benjamin I. Page. 2014. Testing theories of American politics: Elites, interest groups, and average citizens. *Perspectives on Politics* 12(3): 564–581.

Gilligan, Thomas W., and Keith Krehbiel. 1990. Organization of informative committees by a rational legislature. *American Journal of Political Science* 34(2): 531–564.

Glick, David M. 2012. Learning by mimicking and modifying: A model of policy knowledge diffusion with evidence from legal implementation. *Journal of Law, Economics, and Organization* 30(2): 339–370.

Glick, Henry R., and Scott P. Hays. 1991. Innovation and reinvention in state policymaking: Theory and the evolution of living will laws. *Journal of Politics* 53(3): 835–850.

Graham, Erin R., Charles R. Shipan, and Craig Volden. 2013. The diffusion of policy diffusion research in political science. *British Journal of Political Science* 43(3): 673–701.

Gray, Virginia. 1973. Innovation in the states: A diffusion study. *American Political Science Review* 67(4): 1174–1185.

Grossback, Lawrence J., Sean Nicholson-Crotty, and David A. Peterson. 2004. Ideology and learning in policy diffusion. *American Politics Research* 67(4): 521–545.

Hall, Andrew B. 2019. *Who Wants to Run? How the Devaluing of Political Office Drives Polarization*. Chicago: University of Chicago Press.

Hart, Oliver, Andrei Shleifer, and Robert W. Vishny. 1997. The proper scope of government: Theory and an application to prisons. *Quarterly Journal of Economics* 112(4): 1127–1161.

Huber, John D., and Charles R. Shipan. 2002. *Deliberate Discretion? The Institutional Foundations of Bureaucratic Autonomy*. New York: Cambridge University Press.

Jansa, Joshua M., Eric R. Hansen, and Virginia H. Gray. 2019. Copy and paste lawmaking: Legislative professionalism and policy reinvention in the states. *American Politics Research* 47(4): 739–767.

Kahneman, Daniel. 2011. *Thinking, Fast and Slow*. New York: Farrar, Straus and Giroux.

Karch, Andrew. 2007. *Democratic Laboratories: Policy Diffusion Among the American States*. Ann Arbor: University of Michigan Press.

Karch, Andrew. 2012. Vertical diffusion and the policy-making process: The politics of embryonic stem cell research. *Political Research Quarterly* 65(1): 48–61.

Karch, Andrew, and Matthew Cravens. 2014. Rapid diffusion and policy reform: The adoption and modification of three strikes laws. *State Politics and Policy Quarterly* 14(4): 461–491.

Karch, Andrew, Sean C. Nicholson-Crotty, Neal D. Woods, and Ann O'M Bowman. 2016. Policy diffusion and the pro-innovation bias. *Political Research Quarterly* 69(1): 83–95.

Kingdon, John. 1995. *Agendas, Alternatives, and Public Policies*. Boston: Little, Brown.

Kollman, Ken, John H. Miller, and Scott E. Page. 2000. Decentralization and the search for policy solutions. *Journal of Law, Economics, and Organization* 16(1): 102–128.

Koski, Chris. 2010. Greening America's skylines: The diffusion of low-salience policies. *Policy Studies Journal* 38(1): 93–117.

Kruzel, John. 2020. Doctor behind "flatten the curve" urges bipartisan response to outbreak. *The Hill*, March 20. https://thehill.com/policy/healthcare/488559-doctor-behind-flatten-the-curve-urges-bipartisan-response-to-outbreak

LaCombe, Scott, and Frederick J. Boehmke. 2020. Evaluating Approaches for Modeling Learning within Diffusion Episodes. *Sage Handbook of Research Methods in Political Science and International Relations*, eds. Luigi Carini and Robert Franzese, pp. 311–328. London: Sage.

Lau, Richard R., and David P. Redlawsk. 2001. Advantages and disadvantages of cognitive heuristics in political decision making. *American Journal of Political Science* 45(4): 951–971.

Leiser, Stephanie. 2017. The diffusion of state tax incentives for business. *Public Finance Review* 45(3): 334–363.

Linder, Fridolin, Bruce Desmarais, Matthew Burgess, and Eugenia Giraudy. 2020. Text as policy: Measuring policy similarity through bill text reuse. *Policy Studies Journal* 48(2): 546–574.

Maggetti, Martino, and Fabrizio Gilardi. 2016. Problems (and solutions) in the measurement of policy diffusion mechanisms. *Journal of Public Policy* 36 (1): 87–107.

Makse, Todd, and Craig Volden. 2011. The role of policy attributes in the diffusion of innovations. *Journal of Politics* 73(1): 108–124.

Mallinson, Daniel J. 2016. Building a better speed trap: Measuring policy adoption speed in the American states. *State Politics and Policy Quarterly* 16(1): 98–120.

Mallinson, Daniel J. 2021. Who are your neighbors? The role of ideology and decline of geographic proximity in the diffusion of policy innovations. *Policy Studies Journal* 49(1): 67–88.

Maltzman, Forrest. 1998. *Competing Principals: Committees, Parties, and the Organization of Congress.* Ann Arbor: University of Michigan Press.

McConnell, Allan. 2010. Policy success, policy failure, and grey areas in-between. *Journal of Public Policy* 30(3): 345–362.

Meseguer, Covadonga. 2006. Rational learning and bounded learning in the diffusion of policy innovations. *Rationality and Society* 18(1): 35–66.

Miler, Kristina C. 2010. *Constituency Representation in Congress: The View from Capitol Hill.* New York: Cambridge University Press.

Mill, John Stuart. 1859. *On Liberty.* London: Parker and Son.

Mintrom, Michael. 1997. Policy entrepreneurs and the diffusion of innovation. *American Journal of Political Science* 41(3): 738–770.

Mintrom, Michael. 2019. So you want to be a policy entrepreneur? *Policy Design and Practice* 2(4): 307–323.

Mintrom, Michael, and Sandra Vergari. 1998. Policy networks and innovation diffusion: The case of state education reforms. *Journal of Politics* 60(1): 126–148.

Mooney, Christopher Z. 2001. Modeling regional effects on state policy diffusion. *Political Research Quarterly* 54(1): 103–124.

Mooney, Christopher Z. 2020. *The Study of U.S. State Policy Diffusion: What Hath Walker Wrought?* New York: Cambridge University Press.

Nicholson-Crotty, Sean. 2009. The politics of diffusion: Public policy in the American states. *Journal of Politics* 71(1): 192–205.

Nicholson-Crotty, Sean, and Sanya Carley. 2016. Effectiveness, implementation, and policy diffusion: Or "Can we make that work for us?" *State Politics and Policy Quarterly* 16(1): 78–97.

Noll, Roger G., and Andrew Zimbalist. 2011. *Sports, Jobs, and Taxes: The Economic Impact of Sports Teams and Stadiums.* Washington, DC: Brookings Institution Press.

Oates, Wallace E. 1999. An essay on fiscal federalism. *Journal of Economic Literature* 37(3): 1120–1149.

Pacheco, Julianna. 2012. The social contagion model: Exploring the role of public opinion on the diffusion of anti-smoking legislation across the American states. *Journal of Politics* 74(1): 187–202.

Pacheco, Julianna, and Elizabeth Maltby. 2017. The role of public opinion – does it influence the diffusion of ACA decisions? *Journal of Health Politics, Policy, and Law* 42(2): 309–340.

Page, Scott E. 2008. *The Difference: How the Power of Diversity Creates Better Groups, Firms, Schools, and Societies*. Princeton: Princeton University Press.

Parinandi, Srinivas. 2020. Policy inventing and borrowing among state legislatures. *American Journal of Political Science* 64(4): 852–868.

Peterson, Paul E., and Mark C. Rom. 1990. *Welfare Magnets: A New Case for a National Standard*. Washington, DC: The Brookings Institution.

Posner, Paul L. 1998. *The Politics of Unfunded Mandates: Whither Federalism?* Washington, DC: Georgetown University Press.

Rogers, Everett. 2003. *The Diffusion of Innovations*, 5th ed. New York: The Free Press.

Schattschneider, E. E. 1960. *The Semi-Sovereign People: A Realist's View of Democracy in America*. New York: Holt, Rinehart, and Winston.

Schram, Sanford F., and Joe Soss. 2001. Success stories: Welfare reform, policy discourse, and the politics of research. *Annals of the American Academy of Political and Social Sciences* 577(1): 49–65.

Shepherd, Joanna M. 2002. Police, prosecutors, criminals, and determinate sentencing: The truth about truth-in-sentencing laws. *The Journal of Law and Economics* 45(2): 509–533.

Shipan, Charles R., and Craig Volden. 2006. Bottom-up federalism: The diffusion of antismoking policies from U.S. cities to states. *American Journal of Political Science* 50(4): 825–843.

Shipan, Charles R., and Craig Volden. 2008. The mechanisms of policy diffusion. *American Journal of Political Science* 52(4): 840–857.

Shipan, Charles R., and Craig Volden. 2014. When the smoke clears: Expertise, learning, and policy diffusion. *Journal of Public Policy* 34(3): 357–387.

Simon, Herbert A. 1947. *Administrative Behavior, A Story of Decision Processes in Business Organization*. London: Macmillan.

Squire, Peverill. 2007. Measuring state legislative professionalism: The Squire Index revisited. *State Politics and Policy Quarterly* 7(2): 211–227.

Stemen, Don, and Andres F. Rengifo. 2011. Policies and imprisonment: The impact of structured sentencing and determinate sentencing on state incarceration rates, 1978–2004. *Justice Quarterly* 28(1): 174–201.

Tiebout, Charles M. 1956. A pure theory of local expenditures. *Journal of Political Economy* 64(5): 416–424.

Trounstine, Jessica. 2018. *Segregation by Design: Local Politics and Inequality in American Cities*. New York: Cambridge University Press.

Tversky, Amos, and Daniel Kahneman. 1973. Availability: A heuristic for judging frequency and probability. *Cognitive Psychology* 5(2): 207–232.

Tversky, Amos, and Daniel Kahneman. 1974. Judgment under uncertainty: Heuristics and biases. *Science* 185: 1124–1131.

Volden, Craig. 2002. The politics of competitive federalism: A race to the bottom in welfare benefits? *American Journal of Political Science* 46(2): 352–363.

Volden, Craig. 2006. States as policy laboratories: Emulating success in the Children's Health Insurance Program. *American Journal of Political Science* 50(2): 294–312.

Volden, Craig. 2016. Failures: Diffusion, learning, and policy abandonment. *State Politics and Policy Quarterly* 16(1): 44–77.

Walker, Jack L. 1969. The diffusion of innovations among the American states. *American Political Science Review* 63(3): 880–899.

Weyland, Kurt G. 2005. Theories of policy diffusion: Lessons from Latin American pension reform. *World Politics* 57(2): 262–295.

Weyland, Kurt G. 2007. *Bounded Rationality and Policy Diffusion*. Princeton: Princeton University Press.

Wilde, James A. 1971. Grants-in-aid: The analytics of design and response. *National Tax Journal* 24(2): 143–155.

Willison, Charley. 2021. *Ungoverned and Out of Sight: Public Health and the Political Crisis of Homelessness in the United States*. New York: Oxford University Press.

Wiseman, Alan E., and Jerry Ellig. 2007. The politics of wine: Trade barriers, interest groups, and the Commerce Clause. *Journal of Politics* 69(3): 859–875.

Woodward, Bob. 2020. *Rage*. New York: Simon and Schuster.

Yu, Jinhai, Edward T. Jennings, and J. S. Butler. 2020. Lobbying, learning, and policy reinvention: An examination of the American states' drunk driving laws. *Journal of Public Policy* 40(2): 259–279.

Acknowledgments

This study has its genesis in three activities: a series of papers that we (along with other coauthors) have published about policy diffusion, a talk that the Australian and New Zealand School of Government invited one of us to give several years ago to a group of policymakers and academics about why good policies do or do not spread, and an article in *The Monkey Cage* in early 2020 where we first applied some of what we have learned about policy diffusion to the coronavirus pandemic. We thank the many people who have given us feedback in each of these cases, as we have learned much from their insights.

We also thank Marty Jordan, Chinnu Parinandi, and Charley Willison, talented scholars who took the time out of their schedules to read the entire manuscript and give us a set of extremely helpful suggestions. Likewise, we are indebted to Frances Lee, the editor of this series, and the two reviewers, all of whom provided us with invaluable guidance and ideas, helping us produce a much better book. We also benefited greatly from the outstanding research assistance that Francy Luna provided. Finally, we would like to acknowledge Chris Mooney for supplying us with an early copy of *The Study of US State Policy Diffusion: What Hath Walker Wrought?*, a magisterial account of the vast literature on diffusion that we drew upon regularly.

Since this is a work about learning, we wish to thank those from whom we have learned so much. Shipan gratefully dedicates this book to Jerry Loewenberg, John Jackson, and Arlene Saxonhouse – colleagues, friends, mentors, and role models. Volden dedicates it to those who opened the doors to countless learning opportunities – David Brady and Keith Krehbiel at Stanford, Rick Hall at Michigan, Greg Caldeira and Jack Wright at Ohio State, and Eric Patashnik at Virginia – with deepest appreciation.

Cambridge Elements $\equiv$

American Politics

Frances E. Lee
Princeton University
Frances E. Lee is Professor of Politics at the Woodrow Wilson School of Princeton University. She is author of *Insecure Majorities: Congress and the Perpetual Campaign* (2016) and *Beyond Ideology: Politics, Principles and Partisanship in the U.S. Senate* (2009) and coauthor of *Sizing Up the Senate: The Unequal Consequences of Equal Representation* (1999).

Advisory Board
Larry M. Bartels, *Vanderbilt University*
Marc Hetherington, *University of North Carolina at Chapel Hill*
Geoffrey C. Layman, *University of Notre Dame*
Suzanne Mettler, *Cornell University*
Hans Noel, *Georgetown University*
Eric Schickler, *University of California, Berkeley*
John Sides, *Vanderbilt University*
Laura Stoker, *University of California, Berkeley*

About the Series
The Cambridge Elements Series in *American Politics* publishes authoritative contributions on American politics. Emphasizing works that address big, topical questions within the American political landscape, the series is open to all branches of the subfield and actively welcomes works that bridge subject domains. It publishes both original new research on topics likely to be of interest to a broad audience and state-of-the-art synthesis and reconsideration pieces that address salient questions and incorporate new data and cases to inform arguments.

Cambridge Elements ⅀

American Politics

Elements in the Series

A full series listing is available at: www.cambridge.org/core/series/elements-in-american-politics